HAWKER
SIDDELEY
HARRIER

HAWKER SIDDELEY HARRIER

THE WORLD'S FIRST JUMP JET

MARK A. CHAMBERS

The History Press

Cover illustrations
Front: A pair of Royal Navy HMS *Illustrious*-based 800 Naval Air Squadron British Aerospace Sea Harrier FRS.1s hover above the USS *Dwight D. Eisenhower* on 22 October 1984 (US Navy). *Back*: A British Royal Navy FRS.1 Sea Harrier on the flight deck of the USS *Dwight D. Eisenhower* in 1984 (US National Archives at College Park, MD, Still Pictures Branch).

First published 2017

The History Press
The Mill, Brimscombe Port
Stroud, Gloucestershire, GL5 2QG
www.thehistorypress.co.uk

British Library Cataloguing in Publication Data.
A catalogue record for this book is available from the British Library.

ISBN 978 0 7509 6743 3

Typesetting and origination by The History Press
Printed in India by Thomson Press

CONTENTS

ACKNOWLEDGEMENTS

Numerous individuals deserve great thanks for providing crucial support for the completion of this book. First and foremost, sincere thanks go to my loving family – wife Lesa, daughter Caitlyn, and sons Patrick and Ryan – for tolerating my ceaseless words of enthusiasm and providing encouragement and support for this project. Great thanks also go to David Pfeiffer (Civil Records Archivist), Nate Patch (Military Records Archivist) and the entire staff of the Textual Reference Branch of the US National Archives and Record Administration (NARA) at College Park, Maryland; and to Holly Reed and the entire staff of the Still Pictures Branch of the US NARA at College Park, Maryland. Finally, my thanks go to Amy Rigg, Transport Commissioning Editor at The History Press for her unwavering and fantastic encouragement and support in seeing this project through to publication.

INTRODUCTION

In December 1967, the British Hawker Siddeley Harrier, the world's first jump jet, took to the skies for the first time, successfully demonstrating to the world the viability of the jet-powered vertical short take-off and landing (VSTOL) concept. The Harrier went on to become the star of the Royal Navy and Royal Air Force during the Falkland Islands War in Spring 1982. Its American derivative, the McDonnell Douglas AV-8B Harrier II, went on to become the star of the US Marine Corps in Operations Desert Storm, Iraqi Freedom and Enduring Freedom. The Harrier has proven to be a highly versatile and effective strike fighter for several nations for over forty-seven years and will soon be replaced by the stealthy, supersonic Lockheed F-35 Joint Strike Fighter in the UK, US, Italian and Spanish military services. This longevity serves as a testament to the practical design and viability of this truly unique combat aircraft.

1

HAWKER'S CORE: SOPWITH AVIATION

The origins of Hawker Aircraft Ltd date back to the formation and rise to fame of the Sopwith Aviation Company.

SOPWITH AVIATION COMPANY

Perhaps no other British aircraft company became more prominent than the Sopwith Aviation Company during the First World War. Hawker Aircraft Ltd, the manufacturer of the now famous Hawker Siddeley Harrier jump jet, was later formed from the core of the Sopwith Aviation Company following the First World War. In June 1912, the 24-year-old, affluent sportsman Thomas Octave Murdoch Tommy Sopwith (later known as Sir Thomas Sopwith) established the Sopwith Aviation Company in Brooklands, Surrey. Later, Sir Thomas Sopwith set up his aircraft company's headquarters in Kingston upon Thames in London. At the height of the First World War, Sopwith had a total of 5,000 employees. The company produced a total of 16,000 aircraft by the end of the war. In 1917, Sopwith obtained possession of National Aircraft Factory No. 2, further enhancing production of its fighter aircraft. Following the First World War, Sopwith commenced the production of general aviation aircraft, including their Dove, a relative of their famous Pup and Swallow series, and Camel monoplane aircraft. However, the overabundance

The visionary Sir Thomas Sopwith, founder of the Sopwith Aviation Company, in 1911. (Library of Congress, George Grantham Bain Collection)

In 1913, Mr Hawker piloted a Sopwith 'Tabloid' tandem seat trainer to an appearance at Hendon. The Tabloid was one of Sopwith's first aeronautical exploits. (US National Archives at College Park, MD, Textual Reference Branch)

The Sopwith 'Tabloid' featured a side-by-side, two-seat cockpit arrangement. (US National Archives at College Park, MD, Textual Reference Branch)

The Sopwith Gunbus was one of the Sopwith Aviation Company's first aeronautical endeavours of the First World War. It was used mainly as a trainer by Britain's Royal Naval Air Service. (US National Archives at College Park, MD, Textual Reference Branch)

of relatively inexpensive ex-First World War aircraft stymied the lucrativeness of these endeavors. Consequently, Sopwith turned to the motorcycle industry and ABC motorcycles in 1919, manufacturing 400cc flat twin motorcycles, and later bought ABC Motors as well. These civil pursuits, however, were not enough to save Sopwith from dissolution in 1920.

Sopwith Camel

Nevertheless, Sopwith racked up an impressive First World War aircraft production tally. Perhaps its most famous fighter aircraft designed during the war was its Camel design. The Sopwith Camel single-seater fighter biplane made its combat debut in the West in 1917. The aircraft utilised a rotary engine for propulsion and relied on two synched machine guns for armament. The aircraft proved to be quite maneuverable when flown by veteran pilots. Approximately 1,294 enemy aircraft fell victim to the guns of Sopwith Camels, making them the most effective Allied fighter of the First World War. In addition, the Camel excelled as a fighter-bomber as well, often providing crucial close air support to ground forces when needed during the war. The most common Camel variant appeared in the form of the F.1. The Royal Naval Air Service (RNAS) also utilised 2F.1 shipboard variant Camels for missions conducted from aircraft carriers. Sopwith also designed and built the Comic, a night fighter variant of the Camel, as well as the T.F.1 armour-protected ground-attack Camel variant. Numerous two-seat Camel trainers were also built. Several Royal Air Force (RAF) aces flew the Sopwith Camel during the First World War, including Major William Barker, who downed forty-six enemy aircraft/balloons. One of the highest scoring RNAS Sopwith Camel aces was William Lancelot Jordan, of 8 Naval Squadron and later No. 208 Squadron RAF, whose final victory tally in the Camel totaled thirty-nine enemy aircraft. A total of 5,490 Sopwith Camels were produced, with the aircraft type remaining in service until January 1920.

A side view of the first Sopwith Camel F.1 produced. The famous Sopwith fighter would go on to achieve glory during the latter portion of the First World War. (US National Archives at College Park, MD, Textual Reference Branch)

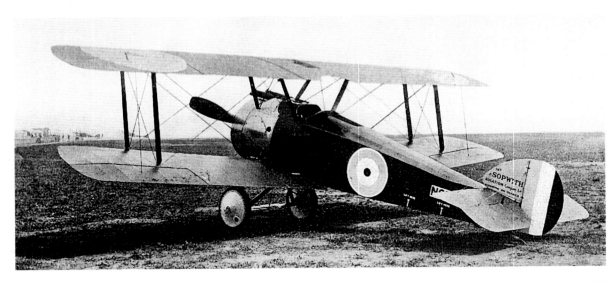

A rear view of the first Sopwith Camel F.1 produced. (US National Archives at College Park, MD, Textual Reference Branch)

The first Sopwith Triplane or 'Tripe' produced. (US National Archives at College Park, MD, Textual Reference Branch)

Sopwith Triplane or 'Tripe'

Another important fighter aircraft produced by Sopwith during the First World War was the famous Sopwith Triplane, which saw service with the RNAS. The Sopwith Triplane became the first combat operational triplane during the First World War. It entered service with No. 8 Naval Squadron in February 1917, before they received their Sopwith Camels. The Sopwith Triplane was an instant hit with its pilots and began to rack up aerial victories immediately. The Triplane possessed a superb climb rate and service ceiling, which enabled it to outclass the German's Albatros D.III. The Sopwith Triplane heavily influenced the design of the famous German Fokker Dr. I Triplane. Perhaps the most famous Sopwith Triplane squadron was the No. 10 Naval

Squadron's 'Black Flight', a Canadian squadron led by Raymond Collishaw. The Black Flight amassed a kill total of eighty-seven German aircraft, with Collishaw personally accounting for thirty-four of these. The Sopwith Triplane was eventually replaced by the Sopwith Camel later in 1917. A total of 150 Sopwith Triplanes were produced during the First World War.

Sopwith 1½ Strutter

In December 1915, Sopwith rolled out its Sopwith 1½ two-seat fighter-bomber, which later saw service as both a fighter-bomber and anti-submarine warfare (ASW) patrol bomber. The aircraft type first became combat operational with No. 5 Wing RNAS, performing bombing missions. While the aircraft did not fare well in combat as a fighter, it did excel as a home defence fighter, operational with the No. 37, No. 44, and No. 78 home defence squadrons. The 1½ Strutters performed admirably for the RNAS, performing bombing missions in the Aegean, Macedonian, and French theatres of combat operations. The RNAS aircraft excelled as shipboard bombers, sortieing from aircraft carriers and other Royal Navy capital warships. Sopwith 1½ Strutters were relegated to training duty by war's end. Nearly 6,000 Sopwith 1½ Strutters were produced during the First World War.

The first Sopwith 1½ Strutter single seat fighter produced. (US National Archives at College Park, MD, Textual Reference Branch)

2

OVERVIEW of HAWKER AIRCRAFT LTD

Following the liquidation of Sopwith, H.G. Hawker Engineering was formed from Sopwith's core. H.G. Hawker Engineering's founders included Tom Sopwith, Harry Hawker, Fred Sigrist and Bill Eyre. H.G. Hawker Engineering ultimately became the predecessor to Hawker aircraft and Hawker Siddeley. Its motto was 'machines that have set a new standard'. And they did indeed set new standards for both aircraft and aircraft production. Hawker's aircraft design and construction philosophy proved to be sound and highly efficient. As stated in Hawker corporate literature:

The essential constructional requirements in any aeroplane, whatever the type, are:

(a)   Ease of production;
(b)   Ease of inspection, and maintenance;
(c)   Reliability;
(d)   Strength combined with lightness; and
(e)   Rigidity with accessibility.[1]

In essence, Hawker made simplicity the cornerstone of its aircraft design philosophy. Most importantly, they wanted their aircraft designs to utilise materials that were readily available and that did not rely on welding techniques. Hence, a unique steel or duralumin tubular aircraft airframe (fuselage) construction system was devised. Hawker aviation pioneer and father of the Harrier concept Sir Sydney Camm played a central role in the conception of this system.

The advantages of procuring Hawker aircraft were realised on an international level. As stated in Hawker corporate literature:

For any country faced with a national emergency it is essential that their Air Force consists of types which can be put into mass production immediately, and for which supplies of raw material and/or spare parts can be obtained without delay or are of such a nature that they can be stored for an indefinite period without fear of deterioration. One of the features of Hawker aircraft is that they are specifically designed with this end in view.[2]

All Hawker aeroplanes were thoroughly and rigorously flight tested by the British Air Ministry at their experimental flight-test facility at Martlesham Heath, England.

HAWKER PIONEER
SIR SYDNEY CAMM

The Hawker Siddeley Harrier was the brainchild of Sir Sydney Camm. Sir Sydney Camm was born on 5 August 1893 in Windsor, Berkshire, England. He was the oldest of twelve children born to Frederick Camm and Mary Smith. Frederick worked as a carpenter and joiner. Young Sydney attended the Royal Free School on Bachelors Acre in Windsor in 1901. He received a Foundation Scholarship in 1906, but dropped out of school in 1908 to pursue employment as an apprentice carpenter. Camm later became interested in aircraft. Both he and his brothers constructed model aeroplanes they provided to Herberts' Eton High Street Shop. They later secretively sold their model aeroplanes at Eton College. Camm eventually founded the Windsor Model Aeroplane Club in 1912.

Prior to the First World War, Camm worked as a shop floor carpenter for the Martinsyde aircraft company in Surrey. He later worked his way up to the drawing office during the war. Following the dissolution of the company in 1921, he worked for George Handasyde. Camm later went to work for the Hawker Aircraft Company, located at Kingston upon Thames, as a senior draftsman in November 1923. The Cygnet served as his initial design project. The Cygnet was a smashing success and contributed to his promotion to chief designer in 1925. Together with Fred Sigrist, Camm pioneered a new type of metal tubular aircraft airframe structures. While working for Hawker, Camm designed fifty-two various aircraft designs. Most notably, he designed the Tomtit, Hornbill, Nimrod, Hart and Fury. All of these aircraft were developed during the 1920s and '30s. In fact, during the 1930s the majority of the aircraft in operational service with the RAF were designed by Camm.

Immediately prior to and during the Second World War, Camm designed fighter aircraft that would serve as the backbone of the RAF's fighter force during the war. These historically significant aircraft included the famous Hawker Hurricane, Typhoon, and Tempest, which helped the RAF wrestle air supremacy from Hitler's Luftwaffe during the Second World War. Camm's aircraft design success continued following the war, as he went on to design the famous Hawker Sea Fury, Seahawk, Hunter, and the revolutionary

The visionary Sir Sydney Camm at the Windsor Model Aeroplane Club in 1915. Camm would eventually play an instrumental role in designing numerous revolutionary aircraft for Hawker Aircraft Ltd during the 1920s, '30s, '40s and '50s, including the famous and now legendary Harrier jump jet. (Royal Air Force)

Harrier jump jet. These aircraft served as warriors for Great Britain during much of the Cold War and during regional conflicts.

Camm resided at his home in Surrey, England with his wife Hilda Starnes, whom he married in 1915, and his daughter, born in 1922. He passed away on 12 March 1966 during a golf outing at the Richmond Golf Course. He was 72 years old at the time of his death. Camm posthumously received the Guggenheim Gold Medal in 1966.

INTERWAR HAWKER AIRCRAFT

The Woodcock

In 1924, the Hawker Woodcock became the first Hawker aircraft to see operational service in Britain's RAF. The aircraft, a single-seater, served as both a day and night fighter. The aircraft utilised a Bristol 'Jupiter' engine for propulsion. The aircraft was made of composite materials and was surprisingly swift. An export version was built by Hawker and sold to the Royal Danish Naval Air Service. The aeroplane, dubbed the 'Danecock', featured an Armstrong Siddeley 'Jaguar' engine and was built at the Copenhagen Dockyard.

Left: The Hawker Woodcock. (US National Archives at College Park, MD, Still Pictures Branch)

Above: A Danish Hawker Woodcock or 'Danecock'. (US National Archives at College Park, MD, Textual Reference Branch)

The Cygnet

The Hawker Cygnet was a light general aviation aircraft designed by Sydney Camm and built in 1924. Two examples, both intended to compete in light aircraft competitions, were produced and flew for the first time in 1924. The Cygnet utilised a 'Cherub' engine and took first and second prizes at the *Daily Mail* Light Aeroplane Efficiency Competition held at Lympne in 1926.

The Horsley

During the 1920s, military aviation planners in Britain expressed the need for a single-engine high-altitude day bomber. Hawker responded by manufacturing the 'Horsley'. This aircraft featured a Rolls-Royce 'Condor' III.A engine as a propulsion source. The aircraft design proved to be highly successful and was specially modified to serve as an all-metal torpedo bomber. The Horsley saw operational duty in Singapore, and with the Greek Naval Air Service and Royal Danish Naval Air Service. The Greek variant was outfitted with a 'Condor' engine, while the Danish variant was equipped with an Armstrong Siddeley 'Leopard' engine. Ease of adaptability for a variety of missions was stressed by Hawker in the Horsley Greek variant, which could be equipped with extra fuel tanks to increase its range. The aircraft was also capable of carrying in excess of twice its ordinary structural weight.

The Hawker Cygnet. (US National Archives at College Park, MD, Textual Reference Branch)

A Hawker Horsley all-metal torpedo bomber. (US National Archives at College Park, MD, Textual Reference Branch)

Above: A Hawker 'Dantorp' torpedo bomber operational with the Royal Danish Naval Air Service. (US National Archives at College Park, MD, Textual Reference Branch)

Right: A Greek Naval Air Service Horsley torpedo bomber. (US National Archives at College Park, MD, Textual Reference Branch)

The Heron

The Hawker Heron served as the company's first fighter aircraft to utilise the metal tubular airframe structure system. Interestingly, this aircraft construction system endured and remained constant in every Hawker design until the company built the Hawker P.1040 jet. The aircraft flew for the first time in 1925 and only one example, the prototype, was produced.

Right: The Hawker Heron fighter prototype, outfitted with a 'Jupiter' engine, at an RAF display in 1925. (US National Archives at College Park, MD, Still Pictures Branch)

The Hedgehog

Design work on the Hawker Hedgehog, a Naval reconnaissance aircraft manned by an aircrew of three, was initiated in 1923 and flew for the first time in 1924. Flight trials of the aircraft were successful, but its performance was no better than contemporary Naval reconnaissance aircraft (the Avro Bison and Blackburn Blackburn) already in service. Therefore, only one example, the prototype, was produced.

Below: The Hawker Heron (left) and Hawker Hedgehog three-seat fleet reconnaissance aircraft at an RAF display in 1925. The Hedgehog was also outfitted with a 'Jupiter' engine. (US National Archives at College Park, MD, Still Pictures Branch)

Bottom: Front view of a Hawker Hornbill fighter. (US National Archives at College Park, MD, Textual Reference Branch)

The Hornbill

In July 1925, a new fighter aircraft designed by Hawker's W.G. Carter and featuring a metal/wood/fabric construction took to the skies over England. The fighter aircraft, the Hawker Hornbill, was never accepted into RAF service because of teething engine/radiator problems as well as suffering from stability/control issues.

Left: Rear view of a Hawker Hornbill fighter. (US National Archives at College Park, MD, Still Pictures Branch)

Below left: A Hawker Hornbill fighter model mounted for tests in a Hawker wind tunnel. (US National Archives at College Park, MD, Still Pictures Branch)

The Harrier Day Bomber

The first aircraft designed and built by Hawker and dubbed 'Harrier' emerged in the form of the Hawker Harrier strike aircraft or day bomber, which flew for the first time in February 1927. The Harrier day bomber was slated to perform torpedo bomber and day bomber roles (carrying conventional gravity bombs). Only one example of the Harrier day bomber, designed by Sydney Camm, was built – this being, once again, the prototype. It was intended to serve as a replacement for the Hawker Horsley coastal torpedo bomber; however, during flight trials, it was found that the Harrier was severely underpowered and incapable of matching the Horsley's superior bomb load. Consequently, the Harrier lost out to the Vickers Vildebeest in the competition to supplant the venerable Horsley.

Above: Front view of the Hawker Harrier day bomber. (US National Archives at College Park, MD, Still Pictures Branch)

Above: Rear view of the Hawker Harrier day bomber. (US National Archives at College Park, MD, Still Pictures Branch)

Right: The Hawker Hawfinch. (US National Archives at College Park, MD, Still Pictures Branch)

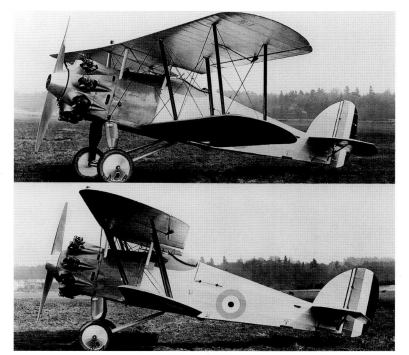

The Hawfinch

In March 1927, another fighter aircraft creation of Sir Sydney Camm took to the skies above England in the form of the Hawker Hawfinch. While the Hawfinch performed admirably, it was not as fast as its primary competitor, the Bristol Bulldog. The Hawfinch also left more to be desired in terms of ease of maintenance. Consequently, it lost out to the more desirable Bristol Bulldog, which served with the RAF for several years into the early 1930s.

The Hornet

In 1929, Sir Sydney Camm and the Hawker design team designed the prototype for the company's famous Fury biplane fighter. This prototype aircraft became known as the Hawker Hornet and featured a new inline Rolls-Royce Kestrel engine. The aircraft was unveiled to the public at the 1929 Olympia Aero Show. In flight trials at Martlesham Heath, the Hornet attained a maximum speed in excess of 200mph. This was over 20mph faster than the Bristol Bulldog II. As a result of its highly successful flight trials, the British Air Ministry decided to procure the Hornet prototype and re-designated the name as 'Fury'. Hawker Furys later entered service with the RAF, becoming that service's premier fighter during the early 1930s.

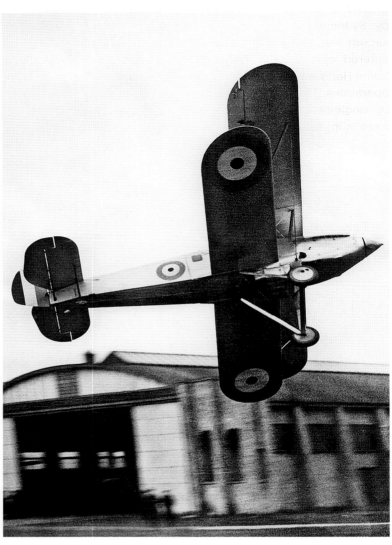

Side view of the Hawker Hornet. (US National Archives at College Park, MD, Still Pictures Branch)

The Hawker Hornet during a flight demonstration. (US National Archives at College Park, MD, Still Pictures Branch)

The Hart

In June 1928, another highly successful Hawker aircraft, designed by Sydney Camm, successfully performed its first flight. The aircraft was the Hawker Hart, a new two-seat light bomber that entered operational service with the Royal Air Force in 1930. Some Harts were produced for the Royal Navy and aircraft carrier operations. The Hart even exceeded performance levels attained by single-seat fighters of the time. Export versions of the Hart were supplied to Sweden, Yugoslavia, Estonia, South Africa and Canada. Some Harts were used as advanced trainers. Hart light bomber variants saw combat during the Abyssinia Crisis (1935–36) in the Middle East and during deployments to the North-West Frontier, British India. A few Harts belonging to the Swedish Air Force saw service with the Finnish during the early years of the Second World War, but they were too obsolescent by then to have any significant impact on the outcome of battle. A total of 1,004 Harts were manufactured.

A radial engine Hawker Hart general-purpose aircraft in flight. (US National Archives at College Park, MD, Textual Reference Branch)

Left: Rear view of a two-seat Hawker Hart fighter in July 1931. This aircraft was equipped with a wind blast deflector for the rear gunner. (US National Archives at College Park, MD, Still Pictures Branch)

Below: Front view of a Hawker Hart, featuring a steam cooled Rolls-Royce F XI B engine. (US National Archives at College Park, MD, Still Pictures Branch)

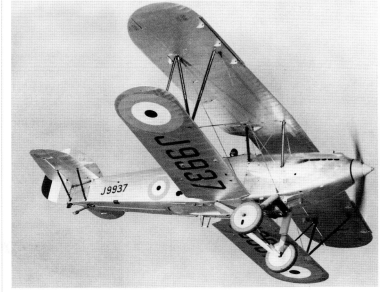

Above: A Hawker Hart day bomber, equipped with a Rolls-Royce F XI B engine, in flight. (US National Archives at College Park, MD, Still Pictures Branch)

Above right: Frontal view of a Hawker Hart two-seat fighter in flight. (US National Archives at College Park, MD, Still Pictures Branch)

Right: A Hawker Hart two-seat fighter during a flight demonstration. (US National Archives at College Park, MD, Still Pictures Branch)

Another view of a Hawker Hart two-seat fighter during a flight demonstration. (US National Archives at College Park, MD, Still Pictures Branch)

The Fury

On 25 March 1931, the revolutionary Hawker Fury biplane fighter successfully performed its first flight. The aircraft proved to be swift and highly manoeuvrable. Upon its entry into RAF operational service in 1931, the Fury became the RAF's first interceptor to possess a maximum attainable speed in excess of 200mph. The Fury also served as the Hart's perfect fighter complement. Export Furies were supplied to the South African Air Force, Spanish Air Force, and Royal Yugoslav Air Force. RAF Fighter Command Furies were not retired from active service until they were supplanted by Gloster Gladiators and more modern Hawker Hurricanes in January 1939. Interestingly, Sir Sydney Camm based his famous Hawker Hurricane monoplane fighter design on its biplane predecessor, the Fury. Approximately 275 Furies were produced.

A formation of RAF Hawker Furies in flight. (US National Archives at College Park, MD, Textual Reference Branch)

Above left: View of a Hawker Fury's Rolls-Royce Kestrel supercharged engine. (US National Archives at College Park, MD, Still Pictures Branch)

Above: A 'Panther' engine equipped Royal Norwegian Air Force Hawker Fury in flight. (US National Archives at College Park, MD, Textual Reference Branch)

Left: Hawker's aircraft structural design philosophy is apparent in this view of the steel tubular fuselage construction of a Hawker Fury fighter. (US National Archives at College Park, MD, Still Pictures Branch)

The Tomtit

In November 1928, the Hawker Tomtit biplane trainer, designed by Sydney Camm, successfully flew for the first time. The Tomtit replaced the RAF's venerable Avro 504N trainer fleet. A total of thirty-five Tomtits were produced.

Above: A Hawker Tomtit blind flying trainer in flight. (US National Archives at College Park, MD, Textual Reference Branch)

Right: Rear view of a Hawker Tomtit trainer. (US National Archives at College Park, MD, Still Pictures Branch)

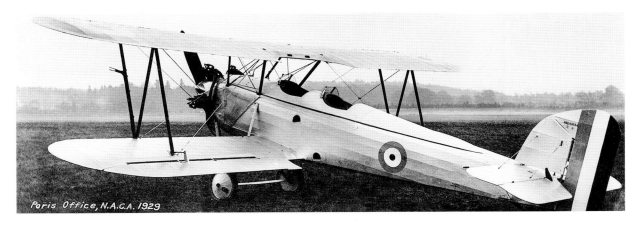

Right: Front view of a Hawker Tomtit in flight. (US National Archives at College Park, MD, Still Pictures Branch)

The Nimrod

In October 1931, the Hawker Nimrod Fleet Air Arm carrier operational fighter, designed by Sydney Camm, successfully performed its maiden flight. The aircraft entered Fleet Air Arm service in 1933, significantly bolstering that service's fighter fleet. The Nimrod was eventually replaced by the Sea Gladiator in May 1939. A total of ninety-two Nimrods were produced.

Below: A Hawker Nimrod fleet defender in flight. (US National Archives at College Park, MD, Still Pictures Branch)

Paris Office N.A.C.A. July 1931

The Osprey

The Fleet Air Arm's Hawker Hart variant became known as the Hawker Osprey, serving as both a fighter and reconnaissance aircraft. The aircraft utilised a Rolls-Royce Kestrel II engine as a propulsion powerplant and was capable of a top speed of 168mph. The aircraft was lightly armed, having one forward-firing .303in Vickers machine gun as well as a .303in Lewis gun. The Osprey was introduced into Fleet Air Arm service in 1932. A total of 103 Ospreys were produced. It remained in Fleet Air Arm service for most of the Second World War, performing as a trainer. In 1936, RAF 701 Squadron Ospreys, operating from RAF Kalafrana, performed anti-submarine warfare (ASW) and anti-piracy duties. Export versions of the Osprey were supplied to the Swedish Air Force, the Portuguese Naval Aviation, and Spanish Republican Air Force.

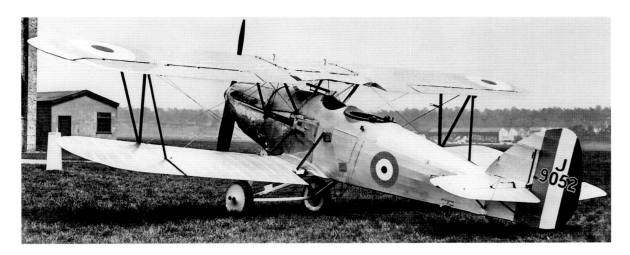

Above: Rear view of a Hawker Osprey fleet observation aircraft. (US National Archives at College Park, MD, Still Pictures Branch)

Left: A Hawker Osprey fleet observation aircraft in flight. (US National Archives at College Park, MD, Still Pictures Branch)

A Hawker Osprey seaplane. (US National Archives at College Park, MD, Textual Reference Branch)

The Audax

The Hawker Audax was developed from the Hart series and was intended for British Army cooperation. The Audax made its maiden flight in late 1931. More than 700 Audaxes were built. The Audax possessed many of the same features found in the successful Hart design. Export versions of the Audax were supplied to the Royal Canadian Air Force, The Royal Indian Air Force, the South African Air Force, the Royal Egyptian Air Force, the Royal Iraqi Air Force, the Imperial Iranian Air Force, and the Southern Rhodesian Air Force. The Audax performed minor roles in the Second World War, serving on the African continent along the Kenya-Abyssinia border. Audaxes also served with the RAF in Iraq. The Audax was retired from active service in 1945.

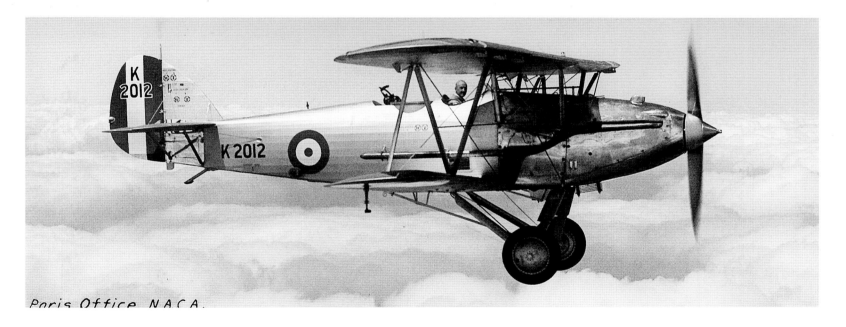

A Hawker Audax British Army cooperation aircraft in flight. (US National Archives at College Park, MD, Still Pictures Branch)

The P.V.3

On 15 June 1934, the Hawker P.V.3 day and night fighter, designed by Sydney Camm, took to the skies over England. The P.V.3 design featured an all-metal airframe and wings covered by fabric. The aircraft's front fuselage was covered by a metal skin. It was armed with four machine guns. The P.V.3 was powered by a Goshawk II engine and excelled, in terms of performance, at its maiden flight trials. The aircraft, however, lost out to the Gloster Gladiator in head-to-head competition and only one P.V.3 was built, that being the prototype aircraft.

Above: Front view of a Hawker I-PV3 fighter. (US National Archives at College Park, MD, Still Pictures Branch)

Left: Side view of a Hawker I-PV3 fighter. (US National Archives at College Park, MD, Still Pictures Branch)

The Hurricane Prototype

Following the demise of the P.V.3 was a competition for an RAF advanced fighter, Sydney Camm designed a new cantilever monoplane design based on the Hawker Fury fuselage. The new aircraft design was slated to receive the Rolls-Royce Merlin engine. It was later decided that the aircraft was to be armed with eight machine guns. The new prototype aircraft, dubbed the 'Hurricane', successfully performed its first flight on 6 November 1935. Hawker test pilot chief Flight Lieutenant George Bulman made the initial flight in the Hurricane prototype K5083. The aircraft was accepted by the British Air Ministry on 26 June 1936 following highly successful RAF trials at Martlesham Heath in February. Sammy Wroath served as test pilot for the RAF trials. The Hurricane entered RAF operational service on 25 December 1937.

The Hawker Hurricane MkI prototype in flight. (US National Archives at College Park, MD, Still Pictures Branch)

Frontal view of the Hawker Hurricane MkI prototype in flight. (US National Archives at College Park, MD, Still Pictures Branch)

The Hawker Hurricane MkI prototype in flight with landing gear down. (US National Archives at College Park, MD, Still Pictures Branch)

Paris Office N.A.C.A. 1936

K5083

Side view of the Hawker Hurricane MkI prototype on the ground.
(US National Archives at College Park, MD, Still Pictures Branch)

SECOND WORLD WAR HAWKER WARRIORS

In the years leading up to and during the Second World War, Sydney Camm designed three notable advanced fighter aircraft that helped wrestle air supremacy from the German Luftwaffe over Europe, North Africa, and the Middle East. These fighter aircraft – the Hawker Hurricane, Typhoon, and Tempest – helped give the Allies the advantage in the air and were fine aeronautical engineering masterpieces. They would go on to amass the greatest number of aerial 'kills' among RAF fighters during the Second World War.

The Hurricane

When Britain went to war against Germany and Italy in Europe and North Africa in 1940, the Hawker Hurricane MkI served as the staple of the RAF's Fighter Command. Watts two-bladed fixed-pitch wooden propellers were utilised in both the prototype and early production Hurricanes for propulsion. In 1939, Hurricanes were outfitted with de Havilland variable-pitch propellers for shorter take-off distances. When the Battle of Britain commenced in 1940, however, Hurricanes utilised constant-speed three-bladed Rotol propellers. The first batch of Hurricanes, designated as MkIs, were produced in June 1936 and the initial four Hurricanes, which utilised Merlin II engines for propulsion, became operational with No. 111 Squadron RAF, based at RAF Northolt, in December 1937. Britain entered the Second World War with 500 operational Hurricane Mk1s assigned to eighteen RAF squadrons.[3]

Above right: An early production Hawker Hurricane MkI flashes its underside while in flight. (US National Archives at College Park, MD, Still Pictures Branch)

Right: Side view of an early production Hawker Hurricane MkI in flight. (US National Archives at College Park, MD, Still Pictures Branch)

One of the first early production Hurricane MkIs on the ground. (US National Archives at College Park, MD, Still Pictures Branch)

The first Hurricane to sport a de Havilland controllable-pitch propeller is demonstrated by Mr P.G. Lucas (right), while Flt.-Lt. P.W.S. (George) Bulman (a well-known Hawker test pilot and director); Mr R.C. Reynell (also a Hawker test pilot, standing behind Bulman); Captain Harold Balfour, M.C., Under-Secretary of State for Air (front right); and Mr F.S. Spriggs, Hawker-Siddeley Group Director, observe. (US National Archives at College Park, MD, Still Pictures Branch)

Hurricanes saw their first combat during the Phoney War on 21 October 1939. During this action, 46 Squadron Hurricanes, based at North Coates airfield, attempted to intercept nine Heinkel He 115B seaplane torpedo bombers of 1/KüFlGr 906 patrolling the waters of the North Sea for Allied shipping targets. A total of four of the German aircraft were downed by the Hurricanes.[4] When the German Blitzkrieg threatened France, Britain responded by deploying four Hurricane squadrons to France in October 1939. While the Hurricanes posted impressive early kill tallies, they began to suffer horrendous losses from more experienced Luftwaffe aces flying Messerschmitt Bf 109Es. During the Battle of France in May 1940, additional Hurricane squadrons were deployed to that country. Hurricanes took a heavy toll on German bombers, but suffered heavy losses against the more maneuverable Bf 109E. It quickly became apparent that the Hurricane was better suited for 'bomber busting' rather than dogfighting.

During the Battle of Britain in 1940, both Hawker Hurricane MkIs and more advanced MkIIs saw combat. In fact, Hurricanes accounted for more than half of the German aircraft destroyed during the battle, the majority of which happened to be bombers. One Hurricane MkI ace, RAF 605 Squadron pilot Archie McKellar, however, managed to shoot down five Bf 109Es in one day on 7 October 1940.[5, 6]

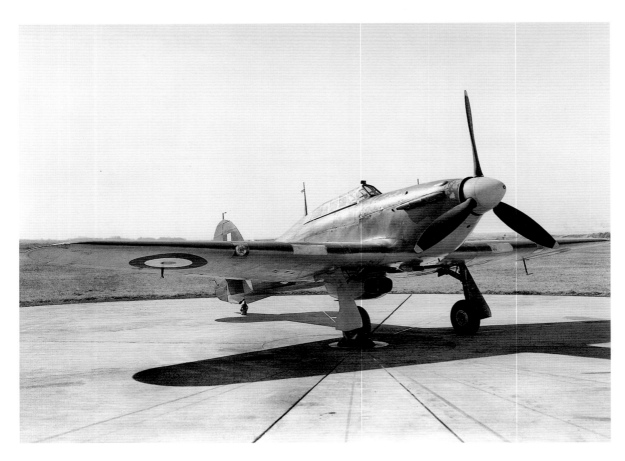

A Hawker Hurricane MkII under evaluation at NAS Anacostia, Washington, DC, United States, on 4 November 1941. (US National Archives at College Park, MD, Still Pictures Branch)

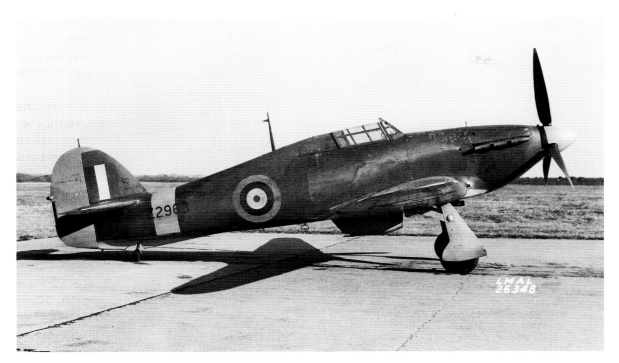

Side view of a Hawker Hurricane MkIIA under evaluation at the National Advisory Committee for Aeronautics' (NACA's) Langley Memorial Aeronautical Laboratory (LMAL) in Hampton, Virginia, United States in late 1941. (US National Archives at College Park, MD, Still Pictures Branch)

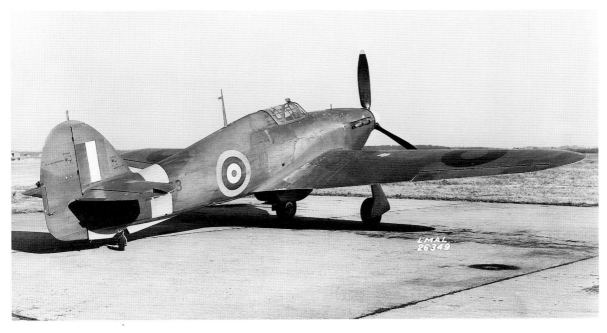

Rear view of a Hawker Hurricane MkIIA under evaluation at the National Advisory Committee for Aeronautics' (NACA's) Langley Memorial Aeronautical Laboratory (LMAL) in Hampton, Virginia, United States in late 1941. (US National Archives at College Park, MD, Still Pictures Branch)

A Hawker Hurricane MkII under evaluation at Wright Field, United States in 1941. (US National Archives at College Park, MD, Still Pictures Branch)

Side view of a Hawker Hurricane MkII under evaluation at Wright Field, United States in 1941. (US National Archives at College Park, MD, Still Pictures Branch)

Side view of a Hawker Hurricane MkII in flight during the Second World War. (US National Archives at College Park, MD, Still Pictures Branch)

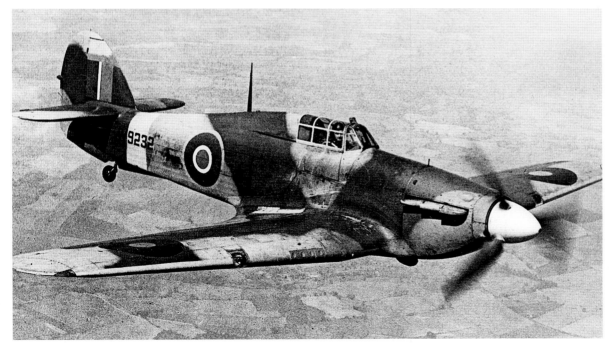

Front view of a Hawker Hurricane MkII in flight during the Second World War. (US National Archives at College Park, MD, Still Pictures Branch)

After the Battle of Britain, the RAF employed new Hurricane MkIIs as night fighters to intercept and shoot down German bombers during the Blitz in 1941. Hurricane MkIICs, equipped with more powerful engines and armament (four wing cannons on each aircraft), excelled in the night intruder role in 1942. Flying a Hurricane MkIIC night intruder, RAF 1 Squadron F/Lt. Karel Kuttelwascher managed to down fifteen German bombers.

Hurricanes fared well in combat when first introduced into the North African theatre of battle in June 1940. The more advanced Hurricanes had no trouble dispatching obsolescent Italian Fiat CR.42 biplane fighters. However, the Hurricanes suffered heavy losses when the Germans introduced Bf 109Es and later Fs into the fray in North Africa. Consequently, the RAF replaced its Hurricanes in North Africa with American-built Curtiss P-40 Tomahawks and Kittyhawks for dogfighting Axis fighters. The Hurricanes were subsequently relegated to fighter-bomber ground-attack duty. During the Battle of El Alamein in October 1942, Hurricane MkIIDs, armed with 40mm cannons, were responsible for the destruction of 39 enemy tanks, 212 armoured personnel carriers and 42 gun emplacements.[7]

Hurricanes performed heroically in defence of the British fortress on the island of Malta. From 1940–42, Hurricanes helped

Left: A Sea Hurricane is test catapulted off a catapult system intended for use aboard British merchantmen and cargo vessels. (US National Archives at College Park, MD, Still Pictures Branch)

Right: A Sea Hurricane is placed on the catapult system aboard a British merchantman vessel during the Second World War. (US National Archives at College Park, MD, Still Pictures Branch)

A formation of Hawker Hurricane MkIIs in flight during the
Second World War. (US National Archives at College Park, MD,
Still Pictures Branch)

turn back Italian and German bombers in the skies over Malta. In 1942, they teamed with carrier-launched Spitfires to thwart a massive German aerial assault on the island fortress. Over 2,500 Hurricanes were supplied to the Soviet Union via the Allied Lend-Lease policy for the defence of Russia. Most of these aircraft were MkIIs.

The Hurricane also made its mark in the Pacific Theatre. RAF 232 Squadron Hurricane MkIIBs distinguished themselves in battle over Singapore in January 1942. Hurricanes laid waste to six Japanese transport ships participating in the Japanese invasion of Sumatra on 14 February 1942. RAF Hurricanes, operating from Ceylon, also gallantly defended Colombo from a large Japanese carrier air strike on 5 April 1942. They once again fought heroically during a Japanese carrier air strike on Trincomalee harbour on 9 April 1942. During the Japanese naval air strike on Trincomalee harbour and China Bay airfield, RAF Hurricanes destroyed three Mitsubishi A6M Zeros and two Nakajima B5N Kate torpedo/strike bombers, as well as damaging an additional ten B5Ns.[8]

Some Hurricanes were navalised during the war, permitting them to operate from ships. Early in the war, to defend convoys from German aerial maritime raiders, a few Sea Hurricanes were modified to be launched via catapults aboard merchantmen ships. These specialised Hurricanes were affectionately dubbed 'Hurricats'. Sea Hurricanes began operating from aircraft carriers in the middle of 1941. They took a heavy toll on German anti-maritime bombers. Perhaps their best combat sortie of the war occurred on 26 May 1944, when Royal Navy Sea Hurricanes, based aboard the escort carrier HMS *Nairana*, downed three Ju 290 maritime reconnaissance aircraft while performing convoy defence duty.[9]

Outstanding RAF Hurricane aces of the Second World War included Douglas Bader, Robert Stanford Tuck, and Peter Townsend. Over 14,500 Hurricanes were produced.

As part of the Lend-Lease Agreement, Britain supplied Russia with several Hawker Hurricane MkIIB fighters. (US National Archives at College Park, MD, Still Pictures Branch)

A British Hurricane, being supplied to Russia, comes in for a landing at a snow-covered Russian airfield, while another Hurricane, in Russian markings, remains parked on the ground, covered by several tarps to prevent ice formation on the aircraft. (US National Archives at College Park, MD, Still Pictures Branch)

A RAF Hurricane MkII, armed for a ground attack mission, in flight during the Second World War. (US National Archives at College Park, MD, Still Pictures Branch)

RAF Desert Hurricanes being prepped for refueling at a
makeshift airfield in Palestine. (US National Archives at College
Park, MD, Still Pictures Branch)

RAF Desert Hurricane MkIIs, such as those depicted in this formation, proved to be instrumental in defeating Rommel and his Afrika Korps in Egypt. (Royal Air Force via the US National Archives at College Park, MD, Still Pictures Branch)

Above: A Hawker Hurricane MkIID (B Flight, No. 6 Squadron RAF) Panzer buster in flight in 1942. The aircraft operated from Shandur, Egypt and was armed with two 40mm Vickers anti-armour cannons. (US National Archives at College Park, MD, Still Pictures Branch)

Right: The pilot of the previously depicted aircraft poses for a publicity photo beside his aircraft back at his base in Egypt. (US National Archives at College Park, MD, Still Pictures Branch)

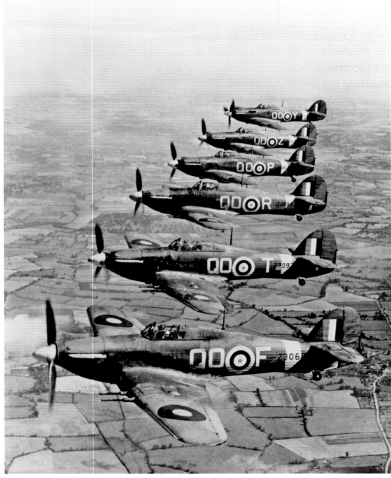

A Hawker Hurricane MkIIC, armed with four 20mm cannons, in flight. (US National Archives at College Park, MD, Still Pictures Branch)

A formation of Hurricane MkIICs in flight. (US National Archives at College Park, MD, Still Pictures Branch)

The Typhoon

After Sydney Camm designed the Hurricane, he sought to design its replacement. The opportunity to develop the Hurricane's replacement presented itself in March 1938 when the British Air Ministry issued Hawker Specification F.18/37, which requested the development of a fighter possessing a speed capability of 400mph at an altitude of 15,000ft. The first Typhoon prototype, P5212, successfully performed its maiden flight on 24 February 1940, despite teething Sabre engine power-plant development issues, with Hawker Chief Test Pilot Phillip Lucas at the controls. More technical problems cropped up in the Typhoon test programme, however, and production was delayed. Consequently, a second Typhoon prototype, P5216, was built and took to the skies on its maiden flight on 3 May 1941. The second Typhoon prototype featured four 20mm Hispano MkII cannons for offensive firepower and performed favorably through its flight test regimen. In the meantime, the Air Ministry requested that Hawker pursue the production of 1,000 Typhoons. Typhoon IB production variants were built based on P5216, with the first production variant, R7576, successfully performing its first flight on 27 May 1941.

When the Luftwaffe introduced its Focke-Wulf Fw 190 into combat in the skies over Europe, it took a heavy toll on the RAF's Spitfire Vs. As a result, the RAF hastily pressed its new Typhoons into service. The Typhoons, combat operational with RAF Nos 56 and 609 Squadrons, suffered heavy losses, mostly due to technical problems. To compound matters, a Typhoon flight-test aircraft experienced a catastrophic structural failure in flight, in which the test pilot perished, in August 1942. More reliability was demonstrated by the Typhoon toward the latter portion of 1942. Typhoon squadrons subsequently were stationed at RAF bases along the south and south-east coasts of England. They were paired with Spitfire MkXII squadrons and performed interception missions in which they managed to destroy several bomb-laden Fw 190s attempting to perform low-altitude nuisance raids on British coastal targets, including airfields. Typhoons also had the distinction of being the first RAF fighters to down the first two Messerschmitt Me 210s over Britain in August 1942.[10] Typhoons also enjoyed another combat outing on 20 January 1943, when the Luftwaffe attempted a daylight bombing mission over London and the British fighters downed four JG 26 Bf 109G-4s and one JG 26 Fw 190A-4.[11]

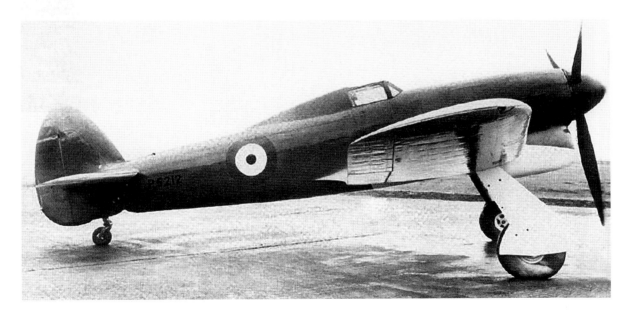

The first unarmed Hawker Typhoon prototype in February 1940. (Hawker-Siddeley Aircraft, British Air Ministry)

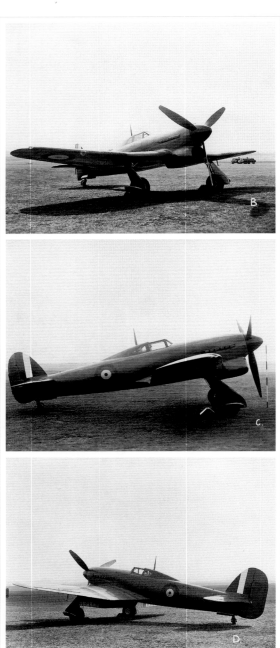

Far left: A Hawker Tornado prototype. It was hoped that the Tornado would replace the Hurricane, but the Tornado lost out to the more successful Typhoon. Only four Tornados were produced, three of which were prototypes. (US National Archives at College Park, MD, Still Pictures Branch)

Left: A machine gun armed Typhoon prototype, outfitted with a Napier 'Sabre' engine. (US National Archives at College Park, MD, Still Pictures Branch)

It became quite apparent to the RAF in 1943 that they desperately needed a fighter-bomber to provide close air support for ground forces. To meet this need, the Typhoon underwent a series of field modifications. The Typhoon's robust engine made it ideal for carrying either two 1,000lb bombs or eight underwing 60lb RP-3 rockets. Typhoon rocket attacks were carried out for the first time by RAF No. 181 Squadron in October 1943 and at year's end, there were a total of eighteen rocket-carrying Typhoon squadrons, comprising the core of the RAF Second Tactical Air Force (2nd TAF) European ground-attack force. Second Tactical Air Force Typhoons went on to perform several memorable and significant sorties during the remainder of the war. One of their finest combat showings occurred in August 1944 during the Battle of the Falaise pocket at Mortain, France. In combat, 2nd Tactical Air Force Typhoons destroyed nine German tanks.[12] Of the 2nd Tactical Air Force Typhoons' contributions to stymieing the German counter-offensive, Supreme Allied Commander Dwight D. Eisenhower stated:

> The chief credit in smashing the enemy's spearhead, however, must go to the rocket-firing Typhoon aircraft of the Second Tactical Air Force ... The result of the strafing was that the enemy attack was effectively brought to a halt, and a threat was turned into a great victory.[13]

Typhoons also performed special ground-attack missions, attacking German High Command headquarters in particular. For example, on 24 October 1944, RAF 146 Typhoon Wing carried out an attack on the German 15th Army high-command headquarters in Dordecht. Seventeen staff officers as well as an additional thirty-six officers perished in the raid, while 15th Army activities remained crippled for the remainder of the war.[14] No. 83 Group RAF, 2nd Tactical Air Force Typhoon 1Bs carried out a series of attacks that ultimately sank the former passenger ships (converted for military purposes) *Cap Arcona*, the *Thielbek* and the *Deutschland* on 3 May 1945.

Group Captain J.R. Baldwin of 609 Squadron, Commanding Officer of 198 Squadron, 146 Typhoon Wing and 123 Typhoon Wing was the RAF's ace with the most aerial combat victories during the Second World War. He was responsible for the destruction of fifteen German aircraft from 1942 to 1944. Overall, during the war, Typhoons accounted for the destruction of 246 enemy aeroplanes.[15] A total of 3,317 Typhoons were produced during the Second World War.

The second Typhoon prototype, armed with four 20mm Hispano MkII cannons. (Hawker-Siddeley Aircraft, British Air Ministry)

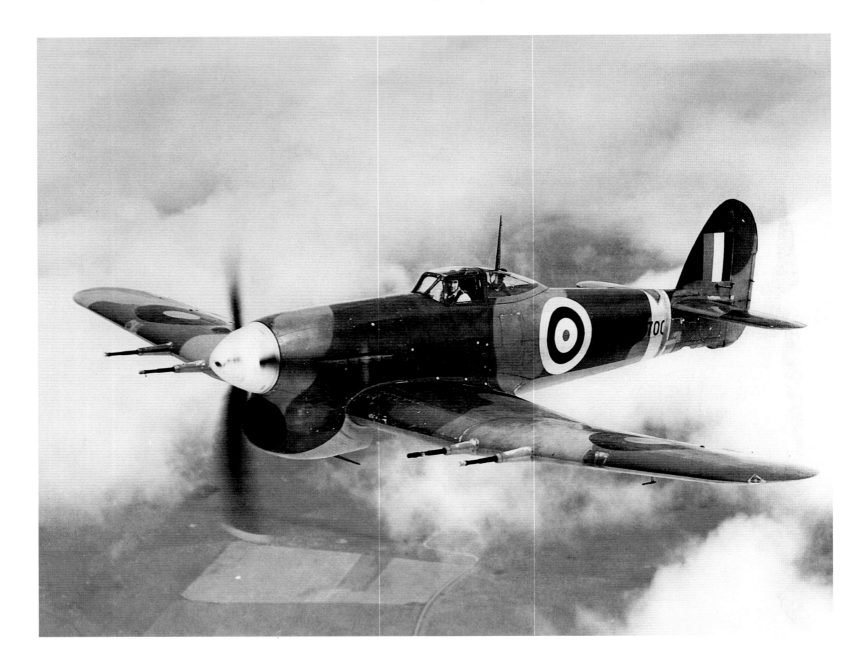

Frontal view of a Hawker Typhoon MkIB in flight. (US National
Archives at College Park, MD, Still Pictures Branch)

Side view of a Hawker Typhoon MkIB in flight. (US National Archives at College Park, MD, Still Pictures Branch)

A Hawker Typhoon MkIB sporting D-Day invasion stripes, signifying the Allied invasion of Nazi-occupied Europe. (US National Archives at College Park, MD, Still Pictures Branch)

A RAF late war Typhoon, featuring a 'bubble top' canopy, is serviced at an aerodrome in Belgium on 29 January 1945. (US National Archives at College Park, MD, Still Pictures Branch)

The Supreme Commander Allied Forces of Liberation, General Dwight D. Eisenhower, observes a RAF late war Typhoon Squadron on the Western Front. The Typhoon he is inspecting is armed with eight RP-3 unguided air-to-ground rockets. (Royal Air Force via the US National Archives at College Park, MD, Still Pictures Branch)

The Tempest

On 2 September 1942, an advanced version of the Typhoon, at first dubbed the Typhoon II but later became known as the Tempest, took to the skies over England for the first time. The Tempest, like its predecessor (the Typhoon), was also designed by Sir Sydney Camm. The Tempest was intended for use by the RAF and was specifically designed to be a better performer than the Typhoon at higher altitudes. The main solution to this problem was to swap out the Typhoon's conventional wing with a newer, thin laminar flow wing. The laminar flow wing was developed through wind tunnel research performed in the United States by a team of researchers, led by Eastman Jacobs, in the low turbulence pressure tunnel (LTPT) at the National Advisory Committee for Aeronautics (NACA), Langley Memorial Aeronautical Laboratory (LMAL), in Hampton, Virginia, in 1940. The laminar flow airfoil was first incorporated in the North American XP-51 Mustang prototype design, and was a major contributor to the success of the US Army Air Forces (USAAF) Mustang air superiority fighter during the Second World War as well as in the Korean War.

The British Air Ministry issued a contract authorising the construction of two prototypes for the design that was to become known as the Tempest on 18 November 1941. The Tempest MkV prototype, *HM595*, successfully performed its first flight on 2 September 1942. The Tempest MkI prototype, *HM599*, took to the skies for the first time on 24 February 1943. During additional flight tests, the Tempest MkI achieved an impressive top speed of 466mph, largely attributable to the incorporation of a Napier

A Hawker Tempest prototype. (US National Archives at College Park, MD, Still Pictures Branch)

A Hawker Tempest in flight in October 1944. (US National
Archives at College Park, MD, Still Pictures Branch)

Sabre IV engine in the design.[16] The Tempest MkIII prototype, *LA610*, successfully performed its maiden flight on 27 November 1944. A total of 400 Tempest Vs and Tempest Is were initially ordered produced by the British Air Ministry in August 1942.[17] These Tempests were powered by Sabre engines.

Tempests were introduced into RAF service in January 1944 and were first used in offensive combat operations over Northern France and the Low Countries in the days leading up to 'D-Day' (the Allied invasion of Normandy) by RAF 150 Wing, assigned to RAF Newchurch. During these offensive combat operations, 150 Wing Tempests conducted high-altitude fighter sweeps, reconnaissance duties, enemy airfield attack missions, attacks on radar installations, strafing raids on ground vehicles, attacks on enemy shipping and attacks on V-1 'buzz bomb' launch sites. The Tempest excelled as an interceptor against low flying V-1 buzz bombs. Tempests accounted for the destruction of 638 out of an overall figure of 1,846 V-1s downed by aeroplanes.[18,19] After participating in Operation Market Garden in September 1944, Tempests, particularly those detached to RAF 122 Wing, routinely dueled with Bf 109Gs and Fw 190s, often outclassing their German foes. By December 1944, Tempests had destroyed fifty-two Luftwaffe fighters, eighty-nine trains and a multitude

A frontal side view of a Hawker Tempest in flight in October 1944. (US National Archives at College Park, MD, Still Pictures Branch)

of German Army armoured ground vehicles. This impressive combat victory tally was amassed at the expense of only twenty Tempest fighters. In 1945, the Tempest gained the distinction of being one of the most effective RAF fighters to duel with the new Messerschmitt Me 262 jet fighter, the world's first combat operational jet fighter. As a matter of fact, the Tempest had registered such an impressive victory tally against the advanced jet fighter that Me 262 airman Hubert Lange once remarked, 'the Messerschmitt Me 262's most dangerous opponent was the British Hawker Tempest–extremely fast at low altitudes, highly-maneuverable and heavily-armed.'[20] The most prolific Tempest ace during the Second World War was an American, Squadron Leader David C. 'Foobs' Fairbanks DFC, active with the Royal Canadian Air Force. Fairbanks registered a victory tally of twelve enemy aircraft destroyed before he was downed himself and became a POW in February 1945.[21]

Engine development projects slated for the Hawker Tornado were later incorporated in the Tempest MkII design. Following a lengthy, technical problem plagued development programme, the Tempest MkII was ready for production in early October 1944. A total of 402 Tempest MkIIs were produced before the war ended, and it was intended to deploy these aircraft to the Pacific Theatre of action. A total of 1,702 Tempests were produced during the Second World War.[22]

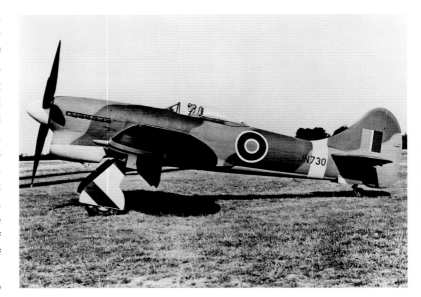

Top: A Hawker Tempest, sporting invasion stripes, on the ground. (US National Archives at College Park, MD, Still Pictures Branch)

Bottom: A Hawker Tempest MkII in flight. (US National Archives at College Park, MD, Still Pictures Branch)

A Hawker Tempest MkII on the ground. (US National Archives at College Park, MD, Still Pictures Branch)

POST-SECOND WORLD WAR HAWKER PRODUCTS

The Sea Fury

During the Second World War, Hawker sought to build on the successes of its Typhoon and Tempest fighters by producing a successor to these highly successful fighters. Sir Sydney Camm, once again, designed this new replacement, which became known as the Fury (the RAF variant) and Sea Fury (the Fleet Air Arm variant) in 1944. The war ended before any Furies or Sea Furies could make it into production. One of the first Sea Fury prototypes to fly, *VB857*, performed a successful maiden flight on 31 January 1946 at the Hawker aircraft production plant at Kingston. Approximately 615 MkII Sea Furies were procured by the Royal Navy.[23]

The Sea Fury went into operational service with Britain's Fleet Air Arm in 1947 and saw extensive combat duty during the Korean War. When Sea Furies entered the war, they were assigned to the 807 Naval Air Squadron and first deployed aboard the HMS *Theseus* in October 1950. These aircraft successfully performed over 250 ground-attack sorties throughout the month of October. By December, the 807 Naval Air Squadron Sea Furies carried out attacks on North Korean bridges, airfields, and railroads. Over 300 additional missions were flown with no losses experienced. Sea Furies also flew combat air patrols and achieved an impressive feat on 8 August 1952, when 802 Squadron Lieutenant Peter 'Hoagy' Carmichael, piloting his HMS *Ocean*-based Sea Fury WJ232, managed to down a Chinese MiG-15 jet fighter. Cuban 'Revolutionary Air Force' Sea Furies were later used against the forces of democracy to intercept and shoot down several Central Intelligence Agency (CIA) Douglas B-26B Invaders during the ill-fated Bay of Pigs invasion in April 1961. Cuban Sea Furies also participated in the sinking of the ammunition ship *Rio Escondido*.[24] The Sea Fury was the final piston-engine fighter to serve the Royal Navy (Fleet Air Arm). It was also one of the world's fastest propeller-driven fighters. A total of 864 Sea Furies were produced.[25]

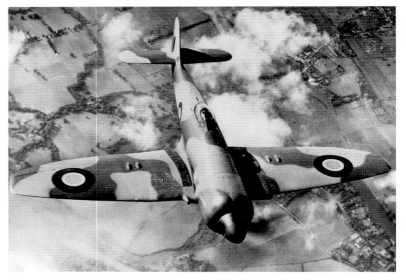

Top: This in-line engine Hawker Fury I was a precursor to the famous Hawker Sea Fury. (US National Archives at College Park, MD, Still Pictures Branch)

Above: A Hawker Fury in flight in 1949. (US National Archives at College Park, MD, Still Pictures Branch)

A Hawker Sea Fury in flight over the Royal Navy fleet. (US National Archives at College Park, MD, Still Pictures Branch)

A Hawker Sea Fury, armed with unguided air-to-ground rockets, takes off from a British aircraft carrier on a ground-attack mission during the Korean War. (US Navy, Naval History and Heritage Command)

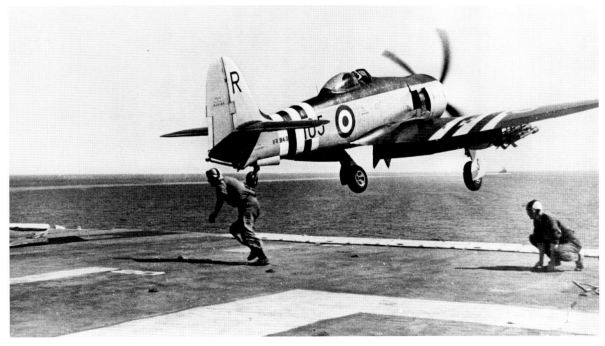

The Sea Hawk

During the latter portion of the Second World War, Hawker pursued the design and development of its first jet-powered aircraft design using its Fury piston-engine fighter as a base design, minus the piston engine. Sydney Camm served as this new jet fighter aircraft's designer. The jet powerplant to be utilised in the design was the Rolls-Royce Nene turbojet engine, to be located in the middle of the fuselage – the fuselage was also to be stretched. The new aircraft design became known as the P.1035. Its design was evaluated by the British Air Ministry in November 1944. Several design modifications were subsequently undertaken in December 1944. The modified design received the designation P.1040. Among the modifications was the provision for four 20mm Hispano-Suiza MkV cannons. Despite the RAF's

waning interest in the project, Hawker pursued the development of a prototype in autumn 1945. In 1946, a naval fighter variant of the P.1040 prototype, known as the P.1046, was proposed by Hawker to the Fleet Air Arm top brass. The Royal Navy was so encouraged with the potential of the design that they requested that three prototypes and a flight-test aircraft be built by Hawker.

Following a tedious flight-test programme that exposed some persistent technical problems with the Sea Hawk prototype designs, the Royal Navy placed an order for production variant Sea Hawks in November 1949. These aircraft were produced at the Hawker Kingston aircraft production facility. Substantial orders were subsequently placed for more Sea Hawks following the commencement of the Korean War. Armstrong Whitworth Aircraft was called upon to supplement Hawker's production

Front view of the Hawker Sea Hawk prototype. (US National Archives at College Park, MD, Still Pictures Branch)

Rear view of the Hawker Sea Hawk prototype. (US National Archives at College Park, MD, Still Pictures Branch)

of the Sea Hawk. The first production variant Sea Hawk, the Sea Hawk F1 (WF143) successfully performed its first flight on 14 November 1951. Sixty Sea Hawk F1s were built. In addition, a total of forty Sea Hawk F2 variants were manufactured.[26] A fighter bomber version of the Sea Hawk, designated the Sea Hawk FB 3, was also produced and became the most prevalent version in operational service. Later, Hawker developed the Sea Hawk FGA6 ground-attack fighter, with a total of over eighty examples being produced.[27]

The Sea Hawk F1 first became operational in 1953 with 806 Squadron assigned to RNAS Brawdy. The Sea Hawk saw its only combat during the Suez Crisis in October 1956, in which Egypt sought control of the Suez Canal in the Middle East and enforced a naval blockade of southern Israel. In response to this act of aggression, England, France, and Israel commenced an invasion

of the geographic territory in dispute, which became known as Operation Musketeer, on 31 October 1956. A total of six Sea Hawk units participated in the military action: two squadrons assigned to the aircraft carrier HMS *Eagle*, two squadrons assigned to the light aircraft carrier HMS *Albion*, and two squadrons assigned to the light aircraft carrier HMS *Bulwark*. The Royal Navy Sea Hawks carried out countless ground-attack sorties against Egyptian ground targets. Their contributions to the Anglo-French invasion were effective, resulting in the reopening of the Straits of Tiran to Israeli maritime commerce and the withdrawal of all ground force and naval combatants from the area of dispute in 1957. Sea Hawks also saw service with the Federal Republic of Germany's (West Germany's) *Bundesmarine*, the Royal Netherlands Navy, and the Indian Navy.

A total of 542 Sea Hawks were produced.

Side view of the Hawker Sea Hawk prototype. (US National Archives at College Park, MD, Still Pictures Branch)

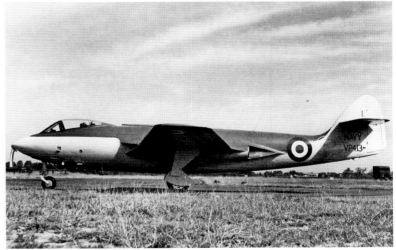

Side view of the Hawker Sea Hawk Royal Navy variant prototype. (US National Archives at College Park, MD, Still Pictures Branch)

The Hunter

At about the same time the Sea Hawk was being developed, Sydney Camm pursued the development of an advanced version of his Sea Hawk design, but equipped with swept wings for enhanced performance. This advanced version of the Sea Hawk became known as the P.1052, which flew for the first time in 1948. While the aircraft design passed flight and carrier trials with flying colours, production was not pursued. Previously in 1946, however, the British Air Ministry issued specification F.43/46, which called for the development of a jet-propelled daylight interceptor, propelled by the new Rolls-Royce Avon turbojet under development at the time. This new jet engine featured an axial compressor design that permitted enhanced power and thrust. Sydney Camm undertook the design duty for Hawker on this project. Later, the Air Ministry modified the specification, now known as Spec. F.3/48. The altered specification called for the development of the previously mentioned aircraft, but possessing a top speed of 629mph at an altitude of 45,000ft,

a greater rate of climb, and four 20mm or two 30mm cannons as armament.[28,29] Camm's product, designated the P.1067, took on the form of today's highly successful Hawker Hunter design. The P.1067 successfully performed its maiden flight over RAF Boscombe Down on 20 July 1951. The aircraft was propelled by an Avon 103 engine. The second prototype Hunter featured a more powerful Avon 107 turbojet and successfully performed its first flight on 5 May 1952. The aircraft was also equipped with production avionics and weapons systems, as well as an additional axial turbojet – the powerful Armstrong Siddeley Sapphire 101. The third Hunter prototype, equipped with a lone Sapphire turbojet engine, successfully performed its maiden flight on 30 November 1952. The Hunter entered production in March 1950, with the first production variant, the Avon 113 turbojet-equipped Hunter F.1, flying successfully for the first time on 16 March 1953. The Hunter MkIII prototype had the distinction of breaking the jet aircraft speed record on 7 September 1953.

Side view of the Hawker Hunter prototype. (US National Archives at College Park, MD, Still Pictures Branch)

The Hawker Hunter prototype in flight. (US National Archives at College Park, MD, Still Pictures Branch)

With its Rolls-Royce Avon jet engine lit, a RAF Hawker Hunter takes off at the Farnborough Air Show, Farnborough RAF Station, England in September 1954. (US National Archives at College Park, MD, Still Pictures Branch)

A Hawker Hunter F MkVI outfitted with a Rolls-Royce reverse thrust unit. (US National Archives at College Park, MD, Still Pictures Branch)

During the historic flight, in which Neville Duke served as pilot, the aircraft attained a speed of 727.63mph in the skies above Littlehampton.[30]

RAF radar-equipped Hunter F.1s became operational in July 1954. The Hunter was intended to replace the aging Gloster Meteors, Canadair Sabres, and de Havilland Venoms still in RAF service. RAF No. 1 and No. 34 Squadron Hunters, flying from RAF Akrotiri in Cyprus, served as fighter escorts for RAF English Electric Canberra bombers bombing ground targets in Egypt during the Suez Crisis in 1956.[31] RAF Hunters once again proved their worth during the 1962 Brunei Revolt, in which the Hunters and RAF Gloster Javelins provided close-air support for British troops in Brunei. RAF Hunters once again provided close-air support for British troops during the Borneo Confrontation. RAF No. 43 and No. 8 Squadrons advanced Hunter FGA.9s and FR.10s took part in combat in Aden in May 1964, supporting

South Arabian States (SAS) and Radfan forces efforts to put down an overthrow attempt by insurgents of the Federation of South Arabia. The Hunter also served as a valuable trainer for both UK and foreign student pilots. Hunters serving with the RAF were eventually replaced by faster English Electric Lightning and McDonnell Douglas F-4 Phantom supersonic fighters in the interceptor/air superiority fighter role and by the Hawker Siddeley vertical short take-off/landing (VSTOL) strike fighter in the ground-attack role. Hunters also performed admirably for the Indian Air Force during the Sino-Indian War in 1962, in which the Indian Hunters held their own, often dominating the opposition in the skies, against Chinese MiGs. Indian Air Force Hunters were also effective in ground-attack operations against Pakistani ground forces during the Indo-Pakistani War in 1971. Hawker Hunters also served with both the Swedish and Swiss Air Forces. Approximately 1,972 Hunters were produced.

A RAF Hawker Hunter F MkIV, sporting Fireflash guided air-to-air missile armament, performs a demonstration flight at the Farnborough Air Show, Farnborough RAF Station, England in August 1956. (US National Archives at College Park, MD, Still Pictures Branch)

A RAF Hawker Hunter MkVI performs a demonstration flight at the Farnborough Air Show, Farnborough RAF Station, England in August 1956. (US National Archives at College Park, MD, Still Pictures Branch)

A formation of RAF Hawker Hunter F MkIVs jet skyward in 1957. (US National Archives at College Park, MD, Still Pictures Branch)

The Nimrod

The British government sought to find a replacement for the Avro Shackleton maritime patrol bomber and anti-submarine warfare (ASW) aircraft and authorised Air Staff Requirement 381 in June 1964. While international aircraft company competition vying to win the production requirement was fierce, the British Government settled on a maritime patrol bomber design, based on the famous de Havilland Comet jetliner design (the world's first jetliner), proposed by Hawker Siddeley. The design was designated HS.801 and became known as the 'Nimrod'. In addition to performing ASW operations, the Nimrod was also capable of performing electronic intelligence gathering (ELINT), airborne early warning, and electronic warfare missions. The Nimrod served as the world's first ASW jet aircraft. The first Nimrod variant, the Nimrod MR1, successfully performed its first flight on 23 May 1967. The RAF was so impressed that it requested forty-six of the aircraft type, which became service operational in October 1969.[32, 33] Other Nimrod variants produced included the R1 (which performed signals intelligence duty), the MR2 (which performed electronic warfare and ASW duties), the AEW3 (which performed Airborne Early Warning duty), and the MRA4 (intended for ASW and search-and-rescue, SAR, missions).

The Nimrod saw its first combat during the Falkland Islands War in April 1982, stationed at Wideawake airfield, Ascension Island. During this deployment, Nimrods flew patrol sorties as well as escort missions, protecting the British naval fleet offshore. In addition, Nimrods performed SAR and communications support sorties for RAF Vulcan bombers participating in Operation Black Buck, as well as ELINT sorties from their base in Punta Arenas, Chile.[34, 35] Nimrods completed a total of 111 combat sorties from their base on Ascension during the Falklands conflict.[36]

Nimrods proved their worth again during Operation Desert Storm. Three Nimrod MR2s participated in Operation Desert Shield, flying from their airbase in Seeb in Oman in August 1990. These aircraft performed maritime patrol sorties above the Gulf of Oman and Persian Gulf. Following the commencement of Operation Desert Storm, the Gulf Nimrod fleet was bolstered by the addition of two more operational aircraft. The Nimrods teamed up with US Navy Lockheed P-3 Orion ASW/maritime patrol aircraft, with the Nimrods conducting patrols at night, while their US partners conducted patrols during the daytime. The Nimrods also vectored Westland Lynx helicopters and Grumman A-6 Intruder attack bombers to the positions of sixteen Iraqi warships that were either sunk or heavily damaged.[37] RAF Nimrod R1s remained operational in the Gulf Region, flying from their base in Cyprus, from August 1990 to March 1991.

Flying from air bases in the Middle East once again, RAF Nimrods were called upon to support Operation Enduring Freedom (the US invasion of Afghanistan) in 2001. These aircraft conducted important ELINT sorties. During Operation Iraqi Freedom in March 2003, RAF Nimrods provided crucial early warning and coalition force guidance capabilities. Nimrods were retired from RAF operational service on 28 June 2011. A total of forty-nine Nimrods were produced.

A RAF Hawker Siddeley MR MkII Nimrod ASW aircraft of 51 Squadron takes off from Incirlik Air Base (AB), Turkey on a surveillance mission during Operation Northern Watch in November 2002. (US National Archives at College Park, MD, Still Pictures Branch)

3

GENESIS of the HARRIER CONCEPT

SHORT SC.1 VTOL TESTBED

The aircraft that contributed most to the design and development of the Hawker Siddeley Harrier was Britain's first attempt at developing a service operational vertical take-off and landing (VTOL) aircraft, the Short SC.1 VTOL technology testbed. The thrust of the SC.1 flight-test programme was to obtain research results and data regarding VTOL flight issues as well as the seemingly difficult transition from vertical to conventional flight mode and back to vertical flight mode. The SC.1 concept originated from a Ministry of Supply (MoS) request that a vertical take-off and landing technology demonstrator be developed in September 1953. The SC.1 concept was deemed worthy of meeting the request specifications and a contract was subsequently let for two research aeroplanes (XG900 and XG905) on 15 October 1954. The unique tailless delta wing research aeroplane design featured four vertically arranged 8,600lb vertical thrust Rolls-Royce RB108 engines that were of the lifting type as well as a single RB.108 engine for cruising in the conventional flight mode. The SC.1 was also the first VTOL aircraft to utilise fly-by-wire control technology. What became known as the 'ground effect' held back the SC.1 in terms of performance, often resulting in a reduction in vertical thrust.

After undergoing a series of engine tests at Short's Belfast, Ireland aircraft production plant, the prototype SC.1 underwent a series of flight tests at the Royal Aircraft Establishment (RAE) Boscombe Down in England. The aircraft successfully performed its initial conventional take-off and landing on 2 April 1957, and in 1958, the second SC.1 prototype successfully performed its maiden tethered vertical flight. Later in 1958, the same aircraft performed a successful untethered vertical flight. The aircraft successfully completed its maiden transition from vertical to conventional flight mode on 6 April 1960. The aircraft made appearances at the Farnborough Airshow in 1958 and 1960, as well as at the Paris Air Show in 1961. Tragedy struck the SC.1 test programme, however, on 2 October 1963, when the second research aeroplane experienced a technical glitch with its control system in flight over Belfast and the aircraft, along with pilot J.R. Green, were lost.[38] Following the reconstruction of the second research aeroplane, the test programme resumed. The SC.1 flight-test programme lasted a little over ten years and yielded a wealth of data that impacted the design of the Hawker Siddeley P.1127, the original forerunner of the Hawker Siddeley Harrier. Technological innovations and flight techniques derived from the SC.1 flight-test programme ultimately benefitted the Harrier programme.

The short SC.1 VTOL test bed performs a hover demonstration flight. (Short via AIAA)

THE BIRTH OF THE HARRIER CONCEPT

The birth of the Hawker Siddeley Harrier began with the conceptualisation of the P.1127 (first Harrier experimental prototype) by Sir Sydney Camm. During the 1950s, numerous European and American aeroplane companies explored, through research, the potential of vertical take-off and landing (VTOL) aircraft. The aircraft companies hoped that the advent of such aircraft would negate the need for a long runway in a contested area of control in times of war and that the new VTOL aircraft could take off and land on either short or makeshift runways. In 1957, the Bristol Engine Company perfected the directable fan jet engine, complete with rotating thrust vectoring nozzles, which featured a combination of Olympus and Orpheus jet engine components.[39, 40] The new directable fan jet engine became known as the Pegasus. The development of the new engine attracted the interest of Hawker's Sydney Camm, who was seeking a successor to the Hawker Hunter fighter. Following the termination of its P.1121 project, Hawker pursued the development of a fighter that utilised the Pegasus engine and met the North Atlantic Treaty Organisation's (NATO's) new Light Tactical Support Fighter specification. In addition, Air Staff Requirement 345 had been issued and requested the development of a V/STOL strike fighter to see service with the RAF.[41] The aircraft design that ultimately emerged on the Hawker Siddeley drawing boards became known as the P.1127. The aircraft, a vertical short take-off and landing (V/STOL) type, was intended for high-speed subsonic strike fighter use and P.1127 prototype serial XP831 underwent extensive ground engine testing at RAF Dunsfold, Surrey, England during the summer and early fall of 1960. The aircraft successfully performed its maiden tethered flight at Dunsfold on 21 October 1960. XP831 successfully performed its maiden free-hover on 19 November 1960. The aircraft successfully performed its maiden conventional flight, with Hawker test pilot Bill Bedford at the controls, on February 1961. The duration of this flight was twenty-two minutes.[42] In May 1961, the same P.1127's original Pegasus engine was swapped out with a more advanced, 12,000-lb thrust Pegasus engine and commenced a new series of hovering trials. The following month, P.1127 XP831 successfully completed a breath-taking transition from vertical flight mode to conventional flight mode. In completing this feat, the aircraft flew the entire runway span at RAF Dunsfold at an altitude of a mere 50m.[43]

P.1127 prototype No. 2, XP836, made its first conventional take-off on 7 July 1961. In September 1961, both XP831 and XP836 successfully performed numerous transitions from vertical to conventional flight mode and from conventional to vertical flight mode.[44] However, military interest in the aircraft had waned by this time. Back on 2 November 1960, Hawker Siddeley received the 'green light' for the production of an additional four prototypes in the hope that the aeroplanes could be developed into viable combat aircraft. In an attempt to fulfill this hope, the 15,000lbf thrust Pegasus 3 engine was developed and incorporated in the designs of the prototypes. In 1963, P.1127 XP831 successfully performed carrier trials aboard the HMS *Ark Royal*, including the completion of a vertical landing aboard the ship.[45, 46] A swept wing was incorporated in the design of the final P.1127, XP984, which also served as a Kestrel (the next Harrier prototype variant)

prototype. Interestingly, during the flight-test programme, some of the P.1127s attained supersonic speeds in shallow dives. So sensitive was the P.1127 design that the first three aircraft crashed during the development programme.

THE HARRIER CONCEPT FACES POSSIBLE TERMINATION BY THE BRITISH PARLIAMENT

During the late 1950s, politicians with socialist leanings controlled the British Parliament and sought to weaken the RAF. Consequently, at the time of the P.1127's conception by Sydney Camm and Hawker project engineer Ralph Hooper, engine powerplant short-comings as well as a general lack of interest in advanced military projects by the aforementioned politicians threatened the continuation of the Harrier's initial developmental programme. As a result, Sydney Camm turned to foreign countries seeking organisations with genuine interest in Hawker Siddeley's P.1127 concept.

HELP FROM AMERICA

NACA/NASA Langley Research Center Rescues the Harrier Programme through Wind-Tunnel and Flight Research Test Programmes

When no potential funding supporters stepped forward, John Stack, the Deputy Director of NACA/NASA Langley Research Center, in Hampton, Virginia, in the United States, learned of this development and informed Hawker Siddeley that his Research Center would conduct research using its research facilities that would prove to the British Government that the Harrier concept would indeed work.

At NASA Langley, P.1127 models were fabricated and tether-tested on a huge rotating crane rigged with control lines (known as the Control Line Facility) that enabled testing of powered models. In addition, a ⅛th-scale free-flight model was built for wind-tunnel research in the centre's massive 30ft × 60ft full-scale tunnel. Finally, a 1/10th-scale peroxide-powered model was fabricated for testing in the centre's transonic wind tunnels. Initial tests of powered P.1127 models on the Control Line Facility showed that a successful transition from vertical to conventional flight mode could be made rapidly. Moreover, wind-tunnel tests using the ⅛th-scale free-flight model in the full-scale tunnel proved the viability and soundness of the vectored-thrust concept in 1960. The Langley wind-tunnel research ultimately helped to persuade the British Government

to provide Hawker Siddeley with the required funding to build the initial P.1127 prototype.

While important Control Line Facility and wind tunnel research was being conducted at NASA Langley, Hawker Chief Test Pilot Bill Bedford and his assistant Hugh Merewether paid a visit to the research center to watch some of the Control Line Facility and wind-tunnel tests, and to log piloting time on the Center's V/STOL flight simulators. Hawker wanted to include NASA in the flight test trials of the P.1127 under the auspices of the International Mutual Weapons Development Programme and the agency sent Langley chief test pilot John P. 'Jack' Reeder as well as Ames chief test pilot Fred Drinkwater to RAF Dunsfold to take

NASA Langley Test Pilot Lee Person poses beside one of the research center's Kestrel flight research aircraft in 1966. (NASA Langley Research Center)

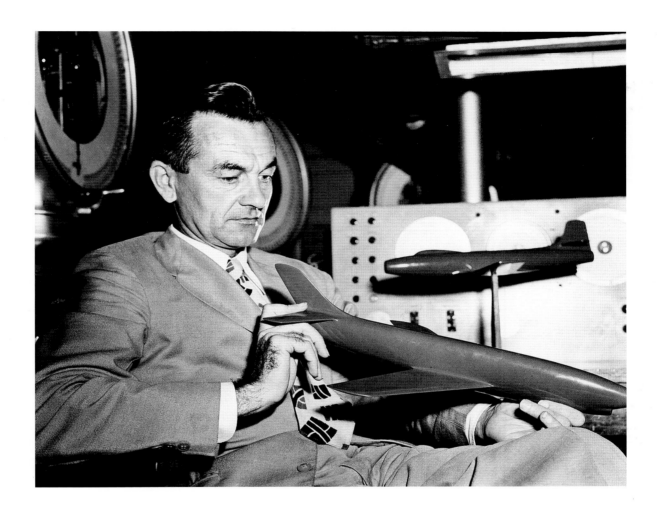

NACA Langley's visionary John Stack. (NASA Langley Research Center)

part in the test trials. In addition to other famous test pilots, the two NASA test pilots focused primarily on the evaluation of the P.1127's vectored thrust in forward flight characteristics and made it known that the aircraft flew superbly.

From 1964 to 1965, the next Harrier prototype variant, the Kestrel, was built. Two Kestrels (XS688 and XS696) initially underwent flight trials. XS688 successfully performed its first flight on 7 March 1964. On 15 October 1964, the Tripartite Squadron, consisting of ten test pilots, was formed to flight test and evaluate the Kestrel. The Tripartite flight-test programme, conducted by Great Britain,

the United States, and West Germany, focused primarily on the vertical short take-off and landing (V/STOL) capability of the Kestrels. After eleven months, a total of 938 successful vertical short take-offs were performed, significantly contributing to the V/STOL aircraft flight operations data and knowledge bases. Following the Tripartite evaluations, six Kestrels were provided to America and received the designation XV-6A. Two XV-6As were assigned to and flight-tested at NASA Langley (Nos 520 and 521). At Langley, NASA test pilot Lee Person became the chief pilot for the Kestrel flight-test programme. The NASA Kestrel flight-test programme focused on investigations of instrument approaches in the aircraft as well as its thrust vectoring in forward flight (VIFF) capabilities. Person found that proper utilisation of the Kestrel's VIFF capability tremendously improved its maneuverability. Indeed, in mock aerial combat studies flown against standard conventional fighters of that time period, the Kestrel often emerged victorious.[47] As once stated by NASA test pilot Lee Person:

> The Kestrel/Harrier type aircraft were my favorite because they did so many things. They took off and landed vertically, they took off and landed like conventional airplanes, they hovered and transitioned from a hovering vehicle into strike type aircraft gracefully and easily. They had handling qualities that were superb ... This airplane was kind of an extension of your thoughts and did just what you wanted it to do. A very light, very precise, and very nimble airplane.[48]

NASA Langley remained extremely active in the development of the American derivative of the Harrier, the McDonnell Douglas (now Boeing) AV-8B Harrier II, in the years to follow. Langley's brilliant aeronautical engineer and visionary Dr Richard T. Whitcomb conceived and developed the supercritical wing, which significantly enhanced aircraft performance and efficiency, during the early 1970s. Supercritical wings were incorporated in the design of the McDonnell Douglas AV-8B Harrier II. Over the

A Hawker Siddeley P.1127 model mounted for tests in the test section of a transonic wind tunnel at NACA Langley. (NASA Langley Research Center)

NACA Langley engineers and technicians display a powered Control Line Facility P.1127 test model at NACA Langley. (NASA Langley Research Center)

To convince British sceptics of the viability of the Harrier concept, NACA Langley tested a ⅛th-scale free-flight P.1127 model in its full-scale tunnel. (NASA Langley Research Center)

NACA Langley engineering test pilot John P. 'Jack' Reeder demonstrates the hovering capability of the Hawker Siddeley P.1127 on a test flight in England in 1962. (NASA Langley Research Center via Jack Reeder)

Jack Reeder disembarks the P.1127 following the successful completion of a test flight. (NASA Langley Research Center via Jack Reeder)

Jack Reeder observes NACA Ames test pilot Fred Drinkwater performing a test flight in the P.1127. (NASA Langley Research Center via Jack Reeder)

AV-8B's history, NASA Langley conducted important wind-tunnel research that proved to be crucial to the aircraft's development programme. NASA Langley generated an extensive AV-8B wing wind-tunnel database, which yielded solutions for improved flap/power systems as well as a supercritical wing that enhanced the short take-off and landing (STOL) load carrying capacity of the Harrier II, representing a marked improvement over earlier AV-8 variants.[49] In 1984, Langley conducted important Spin Tunnel tests of various AV-8B configurations loaded up with various external armament stores.[50]

THE HARRIER'S FIRST FLIGHT (DECEMBER 1967)

At the beginning of 1967, an order for sixty Harrier GR.1s (the GR.1 was the first Harrier production variant) was placed. On 28 December 1967, the Harrier GR.1 successfully performed its maiden flight. So impressed with the Harrier's debut was the RAF that the aircraft type became operational with that branch of Britain's military services on 18 April 1969. On this date, several Harrier GR.1s were acquired by RAF Wittering's Harrier Conversion Squadron.[51] Harrier GR.1 production occurred at two aircraft manufacturing plants (a production plant at Kingston upon Thames in London and another at Dunsfold Aerodrome in Surrey). Trial flights were performed in the skies above Dunsfold. A unique series of tests were conducted at RNAS Yeovilton in 1977 in which the ski-jump carrier take-off technique, later utilised by Royal Navy Sea Harriers, was perfected. Consequently, ski jumps became standard flight deck features aboard Royal Navy aircraft carriers beginning in 1979.[52, 53]

Top: A British test pilot, flying a Hawker Siddeley P.1127, maintains a hover at the Hawker flight test center at RAF Dunsfold. (Imperial War Museum, RAF-T 6794)

Bottom: A pair of Hawker Siddeley P.1127s fly in formation above the scenic English countryside. (Imperial War Museum, RAF-T 6932)

Left: The evolutionary lineage of the Hawker Siddeley Harrier. (NASA Langley Research Center)

Below: NASA Langley test pilot Lee Person maintains vertical flight in a Hawker Siddeley XV-6 Kestrel. (NASA Langley Research Center)

P.1127

KESTREL

HARRIER GR.1,
AV-8A, AV-8S

Right: NASA Langley test pilot Lee Person performing another vertical flight in an XV-6 Kestrel at NASA Langley in 1966. (NASA Langley Research Center)

Below: Lee Person (left) and his mentor Jack Reeder (right) pose in front of NASA Langley's two XV-6 Kestrel flight research aircraft in 1966. (NASA Langley Research Center)

Right: During the early 1980s, the McDonnell Douglas AV-8B Harrier II was the subject of extensive research at NASA Langley Research Center in Hampton, Virginia, United States. Here, an AV-8B model is evaluated in a Spin Tunnel test. (NASA Langley Research Center)

Below: A NASA Langley AV-8B Spin Tunnel test model. (NASA Langley Research Center)

Below right: An AV-8B model mounted on a sting in the test section of the NASA Langley 16ft Transonic Tunnel for tests. (NASA Langley Research Center)

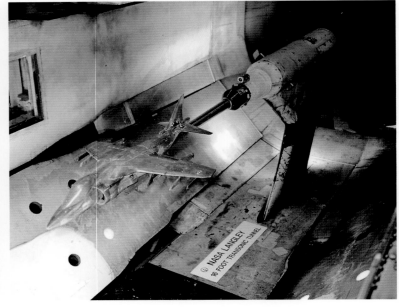

4

BRITISH and AMERICAN HARRIERS BECOME OPERATIONAL

ROYAL NAVY HARRIER VARIANTS

Following the introduction of Hawker Siddeley Harrier GR.1s into operational service with the RAF in April 1969, Hawker Siddeley pursued the development of a Harrier variant for the Royal Navy, which later became known as the Sea Harrier. Early Sea Harriers were designated FRS.1s ('Fighter, Reconnaissance, Strike').[54] An initial order of twenty-four Sea Harrier FRS.1s was placed by the Royal Navy in 1975, with the first becoming operational in 1978.[55,56] The Royal Navy intended to utilise the Sea Harrier as an air superiority fighter and fleet defender. Therefore, all Sea Harriers were outfitted with radars and armed with Sidewinder heat-seeking air-to-air missiles. Sea Harrier pilots greatly benefitted from the aircraft's enhanced navigational carrier landing aids as well as a raised teardrop canopy for improved piloting vision.

In 1977, British Aerospace absorbed Hawker Siddeley. Shortly thereafter, on 20 August 1978, the Sea Harrier prototype successfully performed its first flight at Dunsfold. As a result, the Royal Navy upped the order to thirty-four Sea Harriers. The initial Sea Harrier production variant aircraft was assigned to the 700A Naval Air Squadron, a test and evaluation squadron, at RNAS Yeovilton in 1979. Later in 1980, this test and evaluation squadron was re-designated as the shore-based 899 Naval Air Squadron. 800 Naval Air Squadron Sea Harriers entered service with the Royal Navy in 1981 aboard the HMS *Invincible* and HMS *Hermes*. The remarkable success of the Sea Harrier during the 1982 Falkland Islands conflict also yielded some important operational lessons that were gleaned from its performance. Solutions to potential problems and impediments to satisfactory and maximum aerodynamic performance were addressed in an enhanced variant of the Sea Harrier that became known as the FRS.2 or FA2 Sea Harrier. FA2 development was authorised in 1984, and the prototype aircraft successfully performed its maiden flight in September 1988. Consequently, an order for twenty-nine FA2s was placed by the Royal Navy in December 1988.[57] An additional eighteen 'new build' FA2s were requested by the Royal Navy in 1990.[58] Each individual aircraft cost approximately £12 million. The Royal Navy acquired its initial new-build FA2 Sea Harrier on 2 April 1993.[59]

A line-up of 899 Naval Air Squadron BAe Sea Harrier FRS.1s at Yeovilton Naval Air Station in 1982. (Britpilot)

A RAF Harrier GR1 performs a vertical take-off at RAF Wittering in 1975. (US National Archives at College Park, MD, Still Pictures Branch)

ROYAL AIR FORCE HARRIER VARIANTS

In April 1969, the RAF began replacing its obsolescent Hawker Hunter strike aircraft with new Harrier GR.1s at its base in Wittering. The Harrier GR.1s became operational with No. 1 Squadron. In 1970, two Harrier squadrons became operational at RAF Wildenrath in West Germany. Following the addition of another Harrier squadron at RAF Wildenrath in the years to follow, the three squadrons were transferred to RAF Gütersloh, West Germany. RAF Harriers served primarily as ground-attack/reconnaissance platforms with the full understanding that they could excel in the combat arena as strike fighters to counter an all-out Soviet/Warsaw Pact invasion of Europe. RAF Harriers were also operational in the countries of Norway and Belize. The Harrier GR.1 No. 1 Squadron was assigned to Allied Forces Northern Europe in Norway.

Developed in the late 1960s as one of the original production Harrier variants, the Harrier GR.3 was equipped with enhanced sensors, including a specially designed laser tracker in an extended nose. The aircraft also featured a more powerful Pegasus 11 (Pegasus Mk103) engine. Approximately forty Harrier GR.3s were newly produced, while a total of sixty-two were modified GR.1/GR.1As.[60] The final Harrier GR.3 to be produced was acquired by the RAF in December 1986.[61]

RAF Capt. Tom Plank maintains a hover in a RAF Hawker Siddeley Harrier GR1 before sitting down on a secluded landing area at RAF Wittering, England, on 24 March 1975. (US National Archives at College Park, MD, Still Pictures Branch)

EARLY AMERICAN HARRIER VARIANTS

During the late 1960s, Britain and America formed a Harrier production partnership and discussed the issue of Harrier production in America. Hawker Siddeley and McDonnell Douglas were the two international aerospace companies involved in this new found Anglo-American partnership. However, American Congressman Mendel Rivers as well as the House Appropriations Committee insisted that all AV-8As be produced in the United Kingdom for economical reasons. Therefore, all American AV-8As were sold to the United States by Hawker Siddeley. The United States Marine Corps (USMC) felt the need for an advanced strike fighter in its air fleet and acquired 102 AV-8A as well as eight TAV-8A Harriers from 1971 to 1976.[62] In 1971, the AV-8A became operational with the USMC, which sought usage of the aircraft from ships. Top brass personalities, such as Admiral Elmo Zumwalt, advocated the idea of developing and utilising a 'sea control ship' or light carrier with V/STOL aircraft, such as Harriers, and rotorcraft based aboard. Subsequently, the USS *Guam*, an amphibious assault ship, underwent significant modification to take on the role of such a sea control ship. From 1971 to 1973, the *Guam* participated in operational studies to evaluate the viability and worth of utilising such ships in battle.

Further operational trial testing of AV-8As continued during the mid-1970s, with fourteen Harriers operating from the aircraft carrier USS *Franklin D. Roosevelt* over a six-month period in 1976.[63] These trial tests revealed the Harrier's superior adverse weather operational performance capability. During these formative years of the Marine Corps' Harrier usage philosophy, the USMC decided that in future conflicts it would deploy its Harriers to expeditionary forward battlefront bases to maximise the impact of the Harrier's quick strike capability and enhance the mission rate as well as fuel consumption efficiency. This meant operating from makeshift facilities that were set up at a moment's notice. The USMC also held mock aerial combat missions in which AV-8As were pitted against McDonnell Douglas F-4 Phantom II supersonic fighter bombers. During many matches, the AV-8As came out on top due to their aircrews' usage of the aircraft's unique vectoring-in-forward-flight (VIFF) capability, particularly during close-in combat. These mock aerial combat successes as

Left: A USMC McDonnell Douglas AV-8A Harrier maintains a hover during flight trials at Naval Air Station Patuxent River, Maryland in July 1971. (US National Archives at College Park, MD, Still Pictures Branch)

Right: A USMC AV-8A Harrier, attached to Marine Light Attack Squadron 513, in flight on 2 April 1974. (US National Archives at College Park, MD, Still Pictures Branch)

Above: A USMC AV-8A Harrier, sporting a Sidewinder air-to-air missile, at the Naval Weapons Center, China Lake, California on 15 September 1981. (US National Archives at College Park, MD, Still Pictures Branch)

Right: A USMC AV-8A Harrier performs a vertical take-off from the amphibious assault ship USS *Nassau* (LHA-4) on 1 April 1982. (US National Archives at College Park, MD, Still Pictures Branch)

well as operational testing successes provided the Marine Corps brass with the confidence they needed to proceed with further development of the Harrier.

In 1979, the USMC commenced, in earnest, the AV-8A upgrade programme. The enhanced AV-8A became known as the AV-8C and featured several operational as well as combat system improvements. All AV-8As and AV-8Cs were mothballed in 1987. Their replacement became known as the McDonnell Douglas AV-8B Harrier II, and it became operational in 1985. McDonnell Douglas and British Aerospace entered a partnership to develop and produce significant numbers of AV-8Bs in August 1981. It was originally intended by the two aviation corporate giants to

produce a total of 400 Harrier IIs. Of these, the USMC was to acquire 336 production variants while the RAF was anticipated to acquire sixty production variants. The first developmental Harrier II successfully performed its first flight on 5 November 1981.

The initial production AV-8B variant aircraft was assigned to Marine Attack Training Squadron 203 (VMAT-203) at Marine Corps Air Station Cherry Point (MCAS Cherry Point), North Carolina in December 1983. Another eleven additional aircraft were assigned to Marine Attack Squadron 331 (VMA-331) in January 1985.[64, 65]

These early Harrier II production variants were powered by F402-RR-404A engines, capable of generating 21,450lb thrust. Following 1990, Harrier IIs were fitted with enhanced engines.[66] Despite the highly successful USMC AV-8A and AV-8C Harrier programmes, the Marine Corps lost a considerable number of both aircraft and pilots during the development and operational phases of these aircraft programmes. In all, forty aeroplanes, including AV-8Bs, were lost as well as thirty invaluable pilots throughout the 1970s and '80s.[67]

A USMC AV-8A Harrier is prepped for a sortie aboard the USS Nassau. (US National Archives at College Park, MD, Still Pictures Branch)

USMC AV-8A Harrier mission prep operations aboard the USS *Nassau*. (US National Archives at College Park, MD, Still Pictures Branch)

Another USMC AV-8A Harrier is prepped for a mission aboard the USS *Nassau*. (US National Archives at College Park, MD, Still Pictures Branch)

A USMC AV-8A Harrier lands on the USS *Nassau*. (US National Archives at College Park, MD, Still Pictures Branch)

Above: A USMC VMA-231 AV-8C, armed with Mk82 high-drag bombs, heads out on a sortie at Naval Air Station Fallon, Nevada on 1 January 1983. (US National Archives at College Park, MD, Still Pictures Branch)

Above right: A USMC VMA-231 AV-8C Harrier, armed with napalm bombs, is prepped for a sortie at Naval Air Station Fallon, Nevada in 1983. (US National Archives at College Park, MD, Still Pictures Branch)

Right: A ground crewman arms a Mk82 high-drag bomb on a VMA-231 AV-8C in 1983. (US National Archives at College Park, MD, Still Pictures Branch)

A pair of USMC AV-8A Harriers undergo refueling from a USMC Lockheed KC-130R Hercules in 1978. (US National Archives at College Park, MD, Still Pictures Branch)

An AV-8C Harrier prototype/test aircraft performs flight trials from an amphibious assault ship in 1983. (US National Archives at College Park, MD, Still Pictures Branch)

Below: A USMC VMA-513 AV-8C Harrier performs a vertical take-off from a transport dock ship in 1982. (US National Archives at College Park, MD, Still Pictures Branch)

Right: The AV-8B Harrier II is rolled out from the main McDonnell Douglas aircraft production plant in St Louis, Missouri, on 1 October 1981. (US National Archives at College Park, MD, Still Pictures Branch)

Above: An overhead view of the first AV-8B Harrier II produced. (US National Archives at College Park, MD, Still Pictures Branch)

Left: A test AV-8B Harrier II in flight over Edwards AFB, California on 24 August 1982. (US National Archives at College Park, MD, Still Pictures Branch)

Below: An AV-8B performs a vertical landing on the amphibious assault ship USS *Tarawa* (LHA-1) on 1 August 1986. (US National Archives at College Park, MD, Still Pictures Branch)

Right: A prototype/test AV-8B Harrier II performs a 'Ski Jump' ramp take-off during special testing at the Naval Air Test Center, Patuxent River, Maryland, on 1 April 1983. (US National Archives at College Park, MD, Still Pictures Branch)

Above: A USMC AV-8B Harrier II, loaded up with general-purpose bombs, performs a practice sortie on 1 October 1982. (US National Archives at College Park, MD, Still Pictures Branch)

Right: A USMC AV-8B Harrier II, loaded up with high-drag practice bombs, performs a practice sortie in October 1982. (US National Archives at College Park, MD, Still Pictures Branch)

A USMC AV-8B Harrier II flight demonstration during Airshow
'88 at Marine Corps Base Quantico, Virginia on 11 August 1988.
(US National Archives at College Park, MD, Still Pictures Branch)

A test AV-8B Harrier II in flight above Edwards AFB, California on 1 January 1988. (US National Archives at College Park, MD, Still Pictures Branch)

A view from above an AV-8B (left) and F-21 Kfir on the flight line at Marine Corps Air Station Yuma, Arizona, on 24 March 1988. (US National Archives at College Park, MD, Still Pictures Branch)

61

5

BRITISH HARRIERS GO to WAR in the FALKLANDS

ROYAL NAVY SEA HARRIERS

Combat Operations

When the dispute over the Falkland Islands in the south Atlantic erupted into a full-fledged military conflict in spring 1982, a force of twenty-eight Sea Harriers and fourteen Harrier GR.3s were assigned to the aircraft carriers HMS *Invincible* and HMS *Hermes*, which steamed toward the coastal waters of the islands.[68] British military planners decided that the Sea Harriers would serve as air superiority fighters and fleet defenders, while the RAF Harrier GR.3s would be utilised in the ground-attack role. During the war, Sea Harriers downed a total of twenty Argentine jets, most of which were Mirage III and Mirage V Dagger supersonic jet fighters, while suffering no aerial combat casualties. However, a pair of Sea Harriers fell victims to ground-based anti-aircraft fire, while another four were lost in accidents.[69] A significant reason for the success of the Sea Harrier in aerial combat was its superior manoeuvrability, particularly at close range, over the larger, but faster Argentine jets. In addition, the Royal Navy Sea Harriers were armed with AIM-9L Sidewinder missiles, the latest and world's best short-range, air-to-air missiles purchased from the United States, as well as advanced Blue Fox radar. During

the conflict, Sea Harriers often benefitted from fighter control provided by Royal Navy warships deployed to San Carlos Water.

One factor that hindered Sea Harrier operations was the aircraft's limits on available fuel brought about by the deployment of the British carriers beyond Exocet missile range. However, Sea Harriers still held an advantage over their Argentine aerial opposition in terms of the amount of time they could remain in the air above the combat area, maintaining air superiority. This was also due to the facts that attacking Argentinian aircraft only operated from air bases on the Argentinian mainland and lacked in-flight refueling capability. Another factor that limited the extent of the air superiority maintained by the Sea Harriers was the lack of a British-friendly early warning system or airborne warning and control system (AWACS) asset.

The first known aerial encounter between British and Argentine aerial assets involved Sea Harriers during the morning of 1 May 1982. During this encounter, two Sea Harriers, conducting a combat air patrol (CAP) in the vicinity of Port Stanley, were alerted to the presence of three T-34 Pucará turboprop light attack aircraft in the area. While the Sea Harriers attempted to down the bogies with cannon fire, no kills were registered.

The first meaningful Sea Harrier combat sortie of the war was much more suspenseful, occurring during the afternoon of 1 May. During this aerial encounter, two Sea Harriers were guided via

A view of flight operations aboard the HMS *Hermes* in the South Atlantic during the Falkland Islands War. Three No. 1 Squadron RAF Hawker Siddeley Harrier GR3s and seven Royal Navy British Aerospace Sea Harrier FR1s can be seen on the flight deck. Lt Cdr Smith's 800 Naval Air Squadron Sea Harrier FRS.1, in which he downed an Argentine Skyhawk, is visible in the centre of the photo. (Imperial War Museum, FKD 2300)

Above: HMS *Invincible* weapons crews prepare a Sea Harrier FRS.1 aboard the carrier for a ground-attack mission during the Falklands conflict. The crews are placing a 1,000lb bomb on the aircraft's fuselage underside centerline pylon. (Imperial War Museum, FKD 538)

Right: Flight operations aboard the HMS *Hermes* during the Falklands War. Note the Sea Harrier taking off in the background and the wide variety of armaments on the flight deck. (Imperial War Museum, FKD 127)

a British warship to three Argentine Mirages approaching the British Naval Task Force at high speed. After the Argentine jets evaded, they waited until their British foes returned to their fleet defense duties. Then, the Argentine jets commenced another attack run. This time, however, the British Sea Harriers, once again alerted by the British warship, engaged the Argentinian attackers, downing one of them with an American-made AIM-9L Sidewinder missile. Thus, the Sea Harrier had registered its first aerial kill of the Falkland Islands War.

Left: A pair of 801 Naval Air Squadron British Aerospace Sea Harrier FRS.1s fly a combat air patrol (CAP) in defense of the Royal Navy fleet during the Falklands War. (Imperial War Museum, FKD 2102)

Below: FRS.1 Sea Harriers remained in service with the Royal Navy for several years following the Falklands conflict. Here, three Royal Navy Sea Harriers pay a visit to the USS *Dwight D. Eisenhower* (CVN 69) in 1984. (US National Archives at College Park, MD, Still Pictures Branch)

Left: An aircraft carrier aircraft director guides a British Royal Navy FRS.1 Sea Harrier on the flight deck of the USS *Dwight D. Eisenhower* in 1984. (US National Archives at College Park, MD, Still Pictures Branch)

Below: A British Royal Navy FRS.1 Sea Harrier makes its way to the front of the *Eisenhower*. (US National Archives at College Park, MD, Still Pictures Branch)

Left: A British Royal Navy FRS.1 Sea Harrier takes off from the *Eisenhower*. (US National Archives at College Park, MD, Still Pictures Branch)

Below: A British Royal Navy FRS.1 Sea Harrier performs a high-speed low-level pass for the crew of the *Eisenhower*. (US National Archives at College Park, MD, Still Pictures Branch)

A pair of British Royal Navy FRS.1 Sea Harriers take off on a demonstration flight at the 1982 Farnborough Air Show in England. (US National Archives at College Park, MD, Still Pictures Branch)

Below: A British Royal Navy Sea Harrier FRS.1 at the 1988 Farnborough Air Show in England. (US National Archives at College Park, MD, Still Pictures Branch)

Right: A British Royal Navy Sea Harrier FRS.1 based aboard the HMS *Invincible* (R-05) in 1990. (US National Archives at College Park, MD, Still Pictures Branch)

RAF HARRIERS

Combat Operations

During the Falkland Islands War, ten RAF No. 1 Squadron Harrier GR.3s were assigned to the aircraft carrier HMS *Hermes*.[70] These aircraft underwent extensive modification to operate from aircraft carriers, including being coated with an anti-corrosion sealant and the development of an advanced inertial guidance system that permitted the GR.3s to make vertical landings on the carriers with ease. The aircraft were also outfitted with special transponders that would aid return guidance during night missions as well as flare and chaff dispenser systems. To provide back up for this meager Harrier fleet, two modified container ships, *Atlantic Conveyor* and *Atlantic Causeway*, were pressed into service to accommodate Harriers and rotorcraft in the Falklands Theatre of battle. The primary mission of the Harrier GR.3s was to perform close air support missions for invasion forces as well as strike Argentine ground forces and artillery. As the war progressed, Harrier GR.3s and Sea Harriers were utilised in strike missions on Stanley Airport and airfield.[71] In addition,

A No. 1 Squadron RAF Hawker Siddeley Harrier GR.3 is prepped for a ground attack mission aboard the HMS *Hermes* during the Falklands War. Note the Paveway II laser-guided bombs outfitted on the outboard underwing pylons. (Imperial War Museum, FKD 681)

Harrier GR.3s were modified, their outboard underwing pylons now accommodating Sidewinder missiles, to assist in the air superiority role later in the war. Before the British invasion forces arrived in the Falklands, three GR.3s performed air superiority missions over Ascension Island from 10–24 May 1982. They were eventually relieved by three F-4 Phantom IIs. During the Falklands War, Harriers performed in excess of 2,000 missions, with each aircraft flying six missions each day.[72]

Left: A 1453 Flight RAF Hawker Siddeley Harrier GR.3 at Stanley Airport, Falkland Islands, in 1984. (Petebutt)

Above: A RAF Harrier GR.3 on display at Air Fete '84, held at RAF Mildenhall, England. (US National Archives at College Park, MD, Still Pictures Branch)

Above: The previously depicted RAF Harrier GR.3 maintains a hover at Air Fete '84. (US National Archives at College Park, MD, Still Pictures Branch)

Right: A 1417 Flight RAF Harrier GR.3 in Belize in 1990. (Petebutt)

6

AMERICAN HARRIERS in COMBAT

AV-8BS IN DESERT STORM

Throughout Operations Desert Shield and Desert Storm, USMC McDonnell Douglas (now Boeing) AV-8Bs assigned to the USS *Nassau* and *Tarawa*, and deployed to forward land expeditionary bases, performed training, practice and coalition support missions. When Operation Desert Shield became Operation Desert Storm in mid-January 1991, USMC AV-8Bs were called upon to provide close air support for coalition ground forces. The AV-8B made its combat debut in Operation Desert Storm on the morning of 17 January 1991. This debut originated from a request from a USMC OV-10 Bronco forward air controller for the strike aircraft to take out Iraqi artillery that heavily barraged the town of Khafji, located near the Saudi-Kuwaiti border, and a vital oil refinery. On 18 January 1991, USMC AV-8Bs struck Iraqi ground forces positioned in southern Kuwait. During Desert Storm, AV-8Bs often flew armed recon and coalition support sorties. In fact, a total of eighty-six AV-8Bs flew 3,380 missions, accumulating a total flight time of 4,100 hours for the durations of both Desert Shield and Desert Storm.[73, 74] During this first Persian Gulf War, a total of five AV-8Bs fell victim to Iraqi surface-to-air missiles or SAMs, resulting in the deaths of two USMC pilots. Following the war, famous US Army General Norman Schwarzkopf lauded the AV-8B as one of several advanced US military technology assets that significantly contributed to Coalition victory in Operation Desert Storm. USMC AV-8Bs remained in the Persian Gulf region, assisting Coalition air forces perform patrol duties as part of Operation Southern Watch from 27 August 1992 through 2003. The Marine Corps Harrier IIs operated from various amphibious assault ships deployed to the waters of the Persian Gulf as well as from forward expeditionary bases in Kuwait, including Ali Al Salem Air Base.[75]

Above: A line-up of USMC AV-8B Harrier IIs aboard an amphibious assault ship during Operation Desert Shield in 1990. (US National Archives at College Park, MD, Still Pictures Branch)

Below: The lead aircraft in the previous picture is given the 'all clear' for take-off. (US National Archives at College Park, MD, Still Pictures Branch)

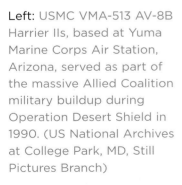

Left: USMC VMA-513 AV-8B Harrier IIs, based at Yuma Marine Corps Air Station, Arizona, served as part of the massive Allied Coalition military buildup during Operation Desert Shield in 1990. (US National Archives at College Park, MD, Still Pictures Branch)

Above: A straight-line formation of the previously depicted aircraft in flight during Operation Desert Shield in 1990. (US National Archives at College Park, MD, Still Pictures Branch)

A USMC AV-8B Harrier II performs a vertical landing aboard the USS *Nassau* during Operation Desert Shield in 1990. (US National Archives at College Park, MD, Still Pictures Branch)

A USMC Harrier II takes off from the amphibious assault ship USS *Nassau* (LHA-4) during Operation Desert Shield in early 1991. (US National Archives at College Park, MD, Still Pictures Branch)

A Mk82 500lb bomb is loaded onto an underwing pylon of a USMC Marine Attack Squadron 331 AV-8B Harrier II, aboard the *Nassau*, in preparation for a ground attack sortie during Operation Desert Storm. The aircraft was based at Marine Corps Air Station Cherry Point, North Carolina. (US National Archives at College Park, MD, Still Pictures Branch)

Above: Iraqi armour, such as this T-55 main battle tank (left) and YW-701 armoured personnel carrier, often fell victim to the wrath of USMC Harrier IIs. (US National Archives at College Park, MD, Still Pictures Branch)

Above right: The burned out hulk of an Iraqi T-72 main battle tank during Operation Desert Storm. USMC Harrier IIs helped wreak havoc on Iraq's T-72 arsenal during Desert Storm. (US National Archives at College Park, MD, Still Pictures Branch)

Above: Evidence of the Harrier II's devastating firepower during Operation Desert Storm. Depicted are the utterly destroyed hulks of an Iraqi BMP-1 infantry battle vehicle and main battle tank. (US National Archives at College Park, MD, Still Pictures Branch)

Above: A USMC Marine Attack Squadron 231 (VMA-231) AV-8B is displayed on the mall commemorating the Coalition victory in Operation Desert Storm on 6 June 1991. (US National Archives at College Park, MD, Still Pictures Branch)

Left: A USMC AV-8B Harrier II performs a vertical landing on the Mall close to the Washington Monument during a National Victory Celebration commemorating the Coalition Victory in Operation Desert Storm on 8 June 1991. (US National Archives at College Park, MD, Still Pictures Branch)

AV-8BS IN ENDURING FREEDOM

For Operation Enduring Freedom, USMC AV-8B Harrier IIs underwent numerous upgrades, such as the installation of the powerful Rolls-Royce Pegasus F402-RR-408 engine, AN/APG-65 radar, and AN/ALQ-28(V) Litening II FLIR/laser designation pod. Immediately following the commencement of Operation Enduring Freedom in 2001, the United States Marine Corps deployed 15th Marine Expeditionary Unit (MEU) AV-8B Harrier IIs aboard its amphibious assault ships, which were stationed near the Pakistani coast in October 2001. A total of four Harrier IIs flew strike sorties in Afghanistan on 3 November 2001. The 15th MEU was supported by the addition of 26th MEU Harrier IIs in the Afghan Theatre of operations during the latter portion of the same month. Eventually, in December 2001, Harrier IIs became combat operational at the Kandahar forward expeditionary base. Additional AV-8Bs supplemented these USMC forces in 2002. In October 2002, the Harrier II programme achieved a combat operational milestone in October 2002, when six VMA-513 squadron Night Attack AV-8Bs became combat operational at Bagram. The Night Attack Harrier IIs proved to be quite effective in conducting reconnaissance/strike sorties against Taliban ground forces largely due to the use of their LITENING targeting pods.

Top: A pair of USMC AV-8Bs prepare for aerial refueling from a USAF KC-10 tanker during Operation Enduring Freedom. (US National Archives at College Park, MD, Still Pictures Branch)

Bottom: A USMC VMA-513 AV-8B, based at MCAS Yuma, Arizona, heads out on a sortie on 9 August 2003 from Bagram Air Base (AB), Afghanistan during Operation Enduring Freedom. Note the GBU-16 laser guided bomb and AN/AAQ-28(V) Litening II Targeting Pod being carried by the aircraft on underwing pylons. (US National Archives at College Park, MD, Still Pictures Branch)

Right: A USMC Harrier II lands on the USS *Nassau* during Enduring Freedom. (US National Archives at College Park, MD, Still Pictures Branch)

Below: Marine Corps armament specialists load laser-guided bombs on a USMC AV-8B during Operation Enduring Freedom. (US National Archives at College Park, MD, Still Pictures Branch)

Below right: A USMC AV-8B lifts off from Bagram AB, Afghanistan in 2003 on a sortie, armed with a 1,000lb laser-guided bomb and a rocket pod, during Enduring Freedom. (US National Archives at College Park, MD, Still Pictures Branch)

Right: A line-up of USMC Harrier IIs aboard the *Nassau* during Enduring Freedom. (US National Archives at College Park, MD, Still Pictures Branch)

Below: A USMC Marine Fighter Attack Squadron Five Four Two (VMFA-542) AV-8B Harrier II prepares to take off on a mission from Ahmed Al Jaber Air Base, Kuwait, during Operation Enduring Freedom on 5 March 2003. (US National Archives at College Park, MD, Still Pictures Branch)

Above: A USMC VMA-513 AV-8B remains at rest at Bagram
Air Base, Afghanistan, during Enduring Freedom. (US National
Archives at College Park, MD, Still Pictures Branch)

AV-8BS IN IRAQI FREEDOM

AV-8Bs once again saw combat two years later in Operation Iraqi Freedom. Prior to this war, the USMC Harrier II fleet was streamlined. During Operation Desert Storm, there were a total of eight Harrier II squadrons (six AV-8B day strike fighters and two AV-8B night strike units). This fleet was pared down to seven Harrier II strike fighter squadrons outfitted with a combination of both night strike fighters and advanced Harrier II+ strike fighters, which boasted new radar systems. In addition to the addition of new Northrop Grumman AN/AAQ-28(V) Litening II precision targeting pods, the USMC Harrier II fleet was equipped with other advanced technologies and weapon systems including GBU-12 laser guided bombs, GBU-38 Joint Direct Attack Munitions (JDAMs), and AIM-120 Advanced Medium-Range Air-to-Air Missiles (AMRAAMs).

During the Second Persian Gulf War, which commenced on 20 March 2003 and lasted until 18 December 2011, Harrier IIs saw extensive combat duty, providing vital close air support for USMC ground forces. During the war, a total of sixty Harrier IIs were assigned to several amphibious assault ships, including the USS *Bonhomme Richard* and *Bataan*. These aircraft flew in excess of 1,000 missions for the duration of the conflict. Some of these AV-8Bs also operated from forward expeditionary land bases, which provided crucial rearming and refueling. Following the war, USMC commander Lieutenant General Earl B. Hailston praised the Harrier IIs for their day-long close air support of ground forces. As stated by Hailston, 'The airplane ... became the envy of pilots even from my background ... there's an awful lot of things on the

Below left: USMC ordnance specialists load GBU-12/B 500lb Paveway II Laser Guided Bombs on a USMC Harrier II aboard the amphibious assault ship USS *Bataan* (LHD 5) during Operation Iraqi Freedom on 25 March 2003. (US National Archives at College Park, MD, Still Pictures Branch)

Below: Another view of the scene depicted in the previous picture. (US National Archives at College Park, MD, Still Pictures Branch)

Left: A USMC AV-8B Harrier II maintains a hover over the USS *Bataan* during Operation Iraqi Freedom on 25 April 2003. (US Navy photo by Photographer's Mate 3rd Class Jonathan Carmichael)

Below left: A USMC AV-8B Harrier II prepares for refueling at a Combat Qualification (Qual Com) site in Iraq during Operation Iraqi Freedom. (US National Archives at College Park, MD, Still Pictures Branch)

Below: Refueling of the previously depicted aircraft at a Qual Com site in Iraq. (US National Archives at College Park, MD, Still Pictures Branch)

Harrier that I've found the Hornet pilots asking me [for] … we couldn't have asked for a better record.'[76]

Harrier IIs conducted in excess of 2,000 combat missions in less than a month during the war. Throughout the war, the Harrier II's Litening II targeting pod proved to be quite lethal to Iraqi ground forces. This fact was highly evident during one particular combat mission in which USS *Bonhomme Richard*-based Harriers decimated a Republican Guard tank battalion as a prelude to the launching of the primary ground-attack on Al Kut.[77] While their effectiveness in battle was impressive, the Harrier IIs were capable of orbiting the battle zone or target area for only fifteen to twenty minutes. Harrier IIs, operating in concert with heavy artillery, offered relentless fire support to ground forces engaged in intense combat against Iraqi insurgents in Fallujah in 2004.

USMC Harrier II pilot Captain Marty Beidell in his aircraft at a Qual Com site in Iraq during Operation Iraqi Freedom on 3 April 2003. (US National Archives at College Park, MD, Still Pictures Branch)

A USMC Harrier II awaiting take-off at a Qual Com site in Iraq during Operation Iraqi Freedom on 3 April 2003. (US National Archives at College Park, MD, Still Pictures Branch)

Above: A USMC AV-8B performs a landing at a Qual Com site in Iraq during Iraqi Freedom. (US National Archives at College Park, MD, Still Pictures Branch)

Top: A USMC VMA-231 AV-8B, carrying Maverick air-to-ground anti-armour missiles, heads out on a mission from Al Asad Air Base, Al Anber Province, Iraq on 1 May 2007. (US National Archives at College Park, MD, Still Pictures Branch)

Above: During Operation Iraqi Freedom, USMC Harriers laid waste to Republican Guard armour, such as this destroyed T-72 main battle tank. (US National Archives at College Park, MD, Still Pictures Branch)

7

MODERN BRITISH and AMERICAN HARRIERS

MODERN BRITISH HARRIERS

Royal Navy Sea Harrier FA2

Advanced Sea Harrier FA2s took part in the war in Bosnia from 1992 to 1995. During the conflict, they conducted air strikes on Serbian ground assets as well as help international forces conduct Combat Air Patrols (CAPs) in Operation Deny Flight and air strikes on the army of Republika Srpska in Operation Deliberate Force. Unfortunately, one of HMS *Ark Royal*'s 801 Naval Air Squadron Sea Harriers fell victim to a Igla-1 surface-to-air missile (SAM) during hostilities on 16 April 1994, but the pilot ejected safely and was recovered by friendly ground forces.[78] HMS *Invincible* Sea Harrier FA2s once again flew CAPs against Federal Republic of Yugoslavia MiGs during Operation Allied Force in 1999. The Sea Harrier FA2's last combat deployment occurred in 2000, when HMS *Illustrious* FA2s saw combat in the skies over Sierra Leone. Naval Air Squadron 801 was the last unit to operate the Sea Harrier before the aircraft type was officially retired in March 2006.

A British Royal Navy FRS MkII Sea Harrier at an air show static display on 24 April 1993. (US National Archives at College Park, MD, Still Pictures Branch)

Left: A side view of a British Royal Navy FRS MkII Sea Harrier at an air show static display on 24 April 1993. (US National Archives at College Park, MD, Still Pictures Branch)

Below: A Royal Navy FA-2 Sea Harrier is positioned toward the HMS *Illustrious*' (RO 6) flight deck elevator while in the Persian Gulf as part of the show of force in South-west Asia on 13 March 1998. (US National Archives at College Park, MD, Still Pictures Branch)

Below: A Royal Navy FA-2 Sea Harrier is positioned on the HMS *Illustrious*' (RO 6) flight deck on 13 March 1998. (US National Archives at College Park, MD, Still Pictures Branch)

Above: An aircraft director guides an FA-2 Sea Harrier aboard the HMS *Illustrious* (RO 6) on 13 March 1998. (US National Archives at College Park, MD, Still Pictures Branch)

Above: A British Royal Navy FA-2 Sea Harrier is prepped for a take-off from the HMS *Illustrious* (RO 6) on 12 March 1998. (US National Archives at College Park, MD, Still Pictures Branch)

Right: A British Royal Navy FA-2 Sea Harrier heads out on a sortie from the HMS *Illustrious* (RO 6) on 12 March 1998. (US National Archives at College Park, MD, Still Pictures Branch)

Royal Air Force Harrier GR.5

At the same time that McDonnell Douglas developed its AV-8B Harrier II, British Aerospace (BAe) pursued the design and development of its British variant, designated the GR.5 Harrier II. The GR.5 represented a significant upgrade over its Harrier GR.1/GR.3 predecessors. The initial developmental GR5 successfully performed its maiden flight on 30 April 1985. The GR.5 became operational with the RAF in December 1989. The GR.5 possessed some dissimilarities from the American AV-8B. These dissimilarities included avionics, weaponry and a distinctly different wing leading edge made of stainless steel. In terms of structural design, the Harrier II utilised advanced composite materials for its fuselage as where its predecessors relied on aluminum alloy for their fuselages. This led to enhanced aerodynamic and performance efficiency.

The Harrier II featured a variety of advanced technological amenities in the cockpit as well, including a head-up display (HUD), multi-purpose colour displays (MPCDs), digitised moveable maps, inertial navigation system (INS), and hands-on-throttle-and-stick system (HOTAS).[79,80] The Harrier II became combat operational with the RAF in Germany. They were strategically stationed there to counter a potential Soviet/Warsaw Pact armoured/infantry invasion of western Europe. Harrier II squadrons were numerous throughout the RAF in late 1990. Although Harrier IIs failed to make their combat debut in Operation Desert Storm, they did debut for combat operations, flying CAP sorties in no-fly zones above Iraq, beginning in 1993 and extending to several years later. All GR.1/GR.3 Harriers were mothballed by 1994.

When war broke out between Croatian and Serbian ethnic factions in Yugoslavia in 1995, an RAF Harrier II unit was deployed to Gioia del Colle Air Base, Italy. These Harrier IIs conducted both attack and recon sorties. In excess of 126 attack missions were performed. Precision-guided weaponry were the weapons of choice by the RAF during the Bosnian War.

Right: A RAF Harrier GR.7 is prepped for a mission aboard the HMS *Illustrious* (RO 6) on 12 March 1998. (US National Archives at College Park, MD, Still Pictures Branch)

Royal Air Force Harrier GR.7

A Harrier II upgrade variant, designated the GR.7 and featuring more powerful Rolls-Royce Pegasus engines as well as TIALD laser designator pods, participated in carrier trials aboard Royal Navy Invincible-class carriers in June 1994. RAF GR.7s began operating from Royal Navy aircraft carriers in 1997, with several of the aircraft type, based aboard carriers deployed to the Persian Gulf, performing combat operational missions over Iraq in 1998. Ship-borne GR.7s once again saw combat duty during the conflict in Sierra Leone in 2000, performing numerous air superiority and recon missions. Shortly after the 1998 Strategic Defence Review, it was decided by the Joint Force Harrier (JFH) Command to conduct and maintain combined RAF Harrier II and Royal Navy Sea Harrier operations.

The RAF deployed twelve Harrier GR.7s, as part of the North Atlantic Treaty Organisation's (NATO's) Operation Allied Force, to take part in combat in Kosovo in 1999. Beginning in April 1999, approximately 870 Harrier II strike missions were performed over a span of seventy-eight days.[81] Harrier GR.7s once again saw extensive combat in 2003 as important parts of Operation Telic.

Operation Telic was Britain's military effort during Operation Iraqi Freedom. The RAF GR.7s performed recon and strike sorties over Southern Iraq targeting and decimating Scud missile launchers. During the Iraq war, American supplied AGM-65 Maverick missiles were routinely used by the GR.7s on Iraqi ground forces and targets. Approximately thirty-eight Maverick Missiles were fired by GR.7s during the conflict.[82] At the height of the war, Harrier GR.7s pounded Iraqi fuel depots, tanks, ships and artillery, particularly during the Battle of Basra. Throughout much of the Iraq war, RAF Harriers performed close air support sorties for allied ground forces on the offensive. RAF and USMC Harrier units were removed from combat in the summer of 2003.

RAF Harrier GR.7s once again proved their worth in the war on terror in Afghanistan. A detachment of six GR.7s relieved a USMC AV-8B squadron based at Kandahar in September 2004.[83] During the initial phase of their Afghan combat deployment, the RAF GR.7s performed 'eminent threat' and recon missions. However, as the war progressed, they were used to perform more strike missions, particularly during the conflict in Helmand province. When requests for close air support reached their peak in 2006, the choice of weaponry for use in strike missions among RAF Harrier pilots was CRV-7 rockets.[84] GR.7 night missions also increased. RAF Harrier GR7s were gradually removed from the Afghan battle theatre, beginning in January 2007. They were relieved by more advanced RAF Harrier GR.9s.

Right: A RAF Harrier GR.7 performs a vertical landing aboard HMS *Illustrious* on 12 March 1998. (US National Archives at College Park, MD, Still Pictures Branch)

Left: A RAF Harrier GR.7 is prepped for a sortie aboard HMS *Illustrious*. (US National Archives at College Park, MD, Still Pictures Branch)

Far right: Another view of the previously depicted aircraft. (US National Archives at College Park, MD, Still Pictures Branch)

Royal Air Force Harrier GR.9

The Royal Air Force Harrier GR.9 and GR.9A represented improvements over the widely used Harrier GR.7. The advanced GR.9s and GR.9As featured improvements in both avionics and weapon systems. The GR9A was outfitted with the more powerful Mk107 Pegasus engine. Development of the GR.9 occurred under auspices of the Joint Update and Maintenance Programme (JUMP). In addition to the addition of more advanced communications software for this Harrier variant, compatibility with AGM-65 Maverick air-to-ground missiles was stressed. Other advanced systems applied to the GR.9 design included the RAF Rangeless Airborne Instrumentation Debriefing System (RAIDS), the Raytheon Successor Identification Friend or Foe (SIFF) system, Paveway smart bombs, Digital Joint Reconnaissance Pod (DJRP), and Sniper targeting pod. The first combat operational RAF Harrier GR.9 squadron was assigned to Kandahar in January 2007, under the command of the NATO International Security Assistance Force (ISAF). In June 2009, all British Harriers were removed from combat in Afghanistan. During the Afghan War, British Harriers performed 8,500 missions and were finally relieved by numerous RAF Tornado GR.4s.[85] All RAF Harriers were retired in March 2011. A total of 143 RAF Harrier IIs were produced.[86]

A RAF Harrier GR.9 on a mission above Afghanistan on 12 December 2008. (USAF photo by Staff Sgt Aaron Allmon)

MODERN AMERICAN HARRIERS

In recent years, USMC Boeing AV-8Bs have been used to combat Islamic State (IS) forces in several Middle Eastern countries, including Iraq and Libya. In July 2014, USMC AV-8Bs, based aboard the USS *Bataan*, flew recon missions in the skies above Iraq, monitoring IS force movements. These Harrier II missions were part of Operation Inherent Resolve, aimed at eliminating IS militants. The first AV-8B Harrier II combat mission, involving the use of force, against IS forces was carried out at the beginning of September 2014, when a 22nd MEU USMC Harrier II laid waste to IS forces, located close to Haditha Dam, Iraq. USMC Harrier IIs, based aboard the USS *Wasp*, participated in airstrikes on the Islamic State of Iraq and Libya's Levant close to Sirte on 1 August 2016. USMC AV-8Bs are slated to be replaced by the stealthy Lockheed Martin F-35 Lightning II joint strike fighter soon.

Above: A USMC VMA-214 AV-8B Harrier II lands at Camp Pendleton, California as part of Exercise Kernel Blitz '97. (US National Archives at College Park, MD, Still Pictures Branch)

Right: A USMC AV-8B Harrier II Plus performs a landing aboard an amphibious assault ship. (US National Archives at College Park, MD, Still Pictures Branch)

USMC VMA-214 Harrier IIs aboard an amphibious assault ship. The aircraft in the foreground is an AV-8B Harrier II and the aircraft in the background is an AV-8B Harrier II Plus. (US National Archives at College Park, MD, Still Pictures Branch)

An Air Test and Evaluation Squadron (VX) 31 AV-8B performs a test flight using a new jet fuel/biofuel mixture in 2011 above the Naval Air Warfare Center Weapons Division, China Lake. (US Navy)

Left: A USMC AV-8B Harrier II Plus lands aboard the USS Kearsarge (LHD 3) on 22 May 2007 while in the Atlantic Ocean. (US National Archives at College Park, MD, Still Pictures Branch)

8

EXPORT VARIANT HARRIERS and the SOVIET VERSION of the HARRIER

EXPORT VARIANT HARRIERS

The AV-8S Matador

The successful demonstration of the Harrier's light aircraft carrier operational capability convinced both the Spanish and Thai navies that they needed the highly versatile V/STOL strike fighter. Britain, through Hawker Siddeley, manufactured an export version of its first generation Harrier aircraft, which became known as the AV-8S Matador. During the mid-1970s, Spain purchased several Matadors from the British government. The United States acted as a 'middle man' in brokering the deal. In 1976, Spanish Matadors, based aboard the Spanish aircraft carrier *Dédalo* – the ex-USS *Cabot*, became operational. Spain and Thailand have now retired their Matador fleets. Thailand purchased a small fleet of Matadors from Spain in 1998 and operated them from their new light carrier HTMS *Chakri Naruebet* during the early 2000s. Although Thailand planned to acquire ex-Royal Navy Sea Harriers, this never came to fruition, and all Thai Matadors were mothballed in 2006.

A Spanish Navy AV-8S Matador performs a mission above the Spanish aircraft carrier *Dédalo* (R01) on 1 June 1988. (US Navy, Lieutenant Commander John Leenhouts)

Left: Frontal view of a Spanish Navy AV-8S Matador in 1977. (US Navy, PH2 James Bishop)

Below: AV-8 Harrier flight operations aboard the Royal Thai Naval HTMS *Chakri Naruebet* (CVH 911) on 3 April 2001. (US Navy, PH3 Alex C. Witte)

The Sea Harrier

India purchased a small fleet of six Sea Harrier FRS Mk51 fleet defenders as well as two T Mk60 Sea Harrier trainers for use in its navy in November 1979. The first three Sea Harrier fleet defenders became operational with the Indian Navy in 1983. A total of ten additional Sea Harriers were acquired in November 1985. In total, approximately thirty Sea Harriers were acquired by the Indian Navy.[87, 88] Indian Navy Sea Harrier pilots trained primarily in England. The Indian Navy's new Sea Harriers replaced its fleet of venerable Hawker Sea Hawk fleet defender aircraft. The Sea Harriers became operational aboard the INS *Vikrant* and INS *Viraat* (originally, the HMS *Hermes*). Indian Navy Sea Harriers often carried advanced weapons, including the Sea Eagle anti-shipping missile developed by Britain, the Matra Magic air-to-air missile developed by France, anti-runway bombs and cluster bombs. However, fifteen IN Sea Harriers were lost in accidents, along with the loss of seven pilots.[89] The IN Sea Harrier fleet underwent an extensive upgrade programme in which fifteen of its Sea Harriers received new Israeli-made Elta EL/M-2032 radars and Rafael 'Derby' medium range air-to-air missiles. IN Sea Harriers flew their last mission from INS *Viraat* on 6 March 2016, with the aircraft type being officially retired from IN service on 11 May 2016. The IN Sea Harriers were replaced by Russian-made MiG 29K/Kub fighters.

Top: Two Indian Navy Sea Harriers in flight with a US Navy F/A-18F Super Hornet on 7 September 2007. (US Navy, Mass Communication Specialist 2nd Class Jarod Hodge)

Bottom: An Indian Navy Sea Harrier performs a take-off from the Indian Navy aircraft carrier INS *Virant* (R22) in 2007. (US Navy)

The AV-8B Harrier II

The Italian Navy had become intrigued with the idea of operating a fleet of Harriers following successful demonstrations of first-generation Harriers aboard various types of ships in the late 1960s. In 1989, the Italian Navy purchased two TAV-8B trainers. So impressed with the Harrier IIs were the Italians that they shortly thereafter purchased sixteen AV-8B Plus aircraft from the United States. The Italian Navy TAV-8Bs were pressed into service first aboard Italian helicopter carriers as well as the light carrier *Giuseppe Garibaldi*. In 1995, the initial Italian-built Harrier II became operational. A small force of three AV-8Bs, based aboard the *Giuseppe Garibaldi*, saw action during Italy's participation in actions to restore calm in a tense Somalia in the middle of January 1995. During these actions conducted over a three-month period, the Italian Navy Harrier IIs flew recon and 'eminent threat' sorties. Italian Harrier IIs made their combat debut in 1999, flying strike missions against the Yugoslavian Army, paramilitary units and infrastructure targets during Operation Allied Force in Kosovo.

These strike missions (in excess of sixty) were launched from the *Giuseppe Garibaldi*.[90] In 2000, the Italian Navy's small Harrier II fleet received upgrades that enabled the aircraft to be armed with AIM-120 AMRAAMs as well as JDAM guided bombs. A fleet of eight Italian Navy Harrier IIs, operating from the *Giuseppe Garibaldi*, saw combat during Operation Enduring Freedom from January through February 2002. Making use of guided munitions, the Italian Navy Harrier IIs flew approximately 131 strike missions in Afghanistan.[91] *Giuseppe Garibaldi*-based Harrier IIs, as well as Italian Typhoon Eurofighters, saw combat once again in 2011 as part of Operation Unified Protector carried out against Libya. During this conflict, Italian Navy Harrier IIs flew recon and strike missions in Libya. The aircraft made use of Litening targeting pods and were equipped with AIM 120 AMRAAMs and AIM-9 Sidewinders. The small fleet of Italian Navy Harrier IIs delivered a total of 160 precision-guided munitions to their targets during the conflict.[92]

In March 1983, Spain placed an order for twelve AV-8Bs. This made Spain the first export Harrier II operator. The Spanish Navy's

Italian Navy TAV-8B Harrier II flight operations aboard the carrier *Guiseppe Garibaldi* (C-551) as part of the joint exercise Dragon Hammer 1992. (US National Archives at College Park, MD, Still Pictures Branch)

Harrier IIs became known as VA-2 Matador IIs or EAV-8Bs. The initial three Matador IIs arrived at Naval Station Rota on 6 October 1987, with all EAV-8Bs arriving in Spain by 1988. The Spanish aircraft carrier *Principe de Asturias* was specially modified to accommodate the EAV-8Bs. Spain purchased eight EAV-8B Plus Matador IIs as well as a single TAV-8B two-seat trainer from the United States in March 1993, with the aircraft arriving in Spain in 1996. In 2000, Boeing and NAVAIR remanufactured five EAV-8Bs.[93] These rebuilt aeroplanes could now be equipped with four AIM-120 AMRAAMs and featured new radars, avionics, and engines. The Spanish EAV-8B fleet participated in Operation Deny Flight, which involved flying CAP missions within the no-fly zone in the skies above Bosnia and Herzegovina. The Spanish Navy currently operates a modest EAV-8B fleet from only one ship, the amphibious assault ship *Juan Carlos*.

Two Italian Navy AV-8B Harrier II Pluses in flight with a US Navy F/A-18C Hornet in 2004. (US National Archives at College Park, MD, Still Pictures Branch)

THE SOVIET VERSION OF THE HARRIER

The Yakovlev Yak-38 Forger

In April 1970, the Soviet Union developed the prototype of a VTOL aircraft that bore a striking semblance to the British Hawker Siddeley Harrier. The aircraft, developed by the A.S. Yakovlev Design Bureau JSC, became known as the Yak-38 Forger and was evolved from the Yakovlev Yak-36, which operated from land bases. Like the British Harrier, the Soviet Forger was intended to operate at speeds near the speed of sound (Mach 1). Unlike the Harrier, however, the Forger was equipped with an automatic ejection seat that automatically ejected the pilot in the event of one of the take-off engines shutting down unexpectedly.

The Forger was powered by one Tumansky R-28 V-300 turbojet, capable of producing 15,000lb of thrust, and two Rybinsk RD-38 turbojets, each capable of producing 7,870lb of thrust. The aircraft also featured armament consisting of GSU-23L 23mm or GP-9 gun pods, housed in a pair of UPK-23-250 pods carried on underwing pylons; various air-to-ground rockets; a pair of anti-shipping or air-to-surface Kh-23 (AS-7 Kerry) missiles; a pair of R-60 or R-60M (AA-8 Aphid) air-to-air missiles, outfitted on underwing pylons; two FAB-500/four FAB-250 gravity bombs; two ZB-500 incendiary bombs; two nuclear RN-28 bombs; or fuel tanks. The Yak-38 successfully performed its first flight in 1971. It became operational with the Soviet Navy in 1976.

The Yak-38 first became operational with the 279 *OKShAP* (*Otdelny Korabelny Shturmovoy Aviatsionny Polk*, Independent Shipboard Attack Air Regiment). These aircraft operated from Saki in the Crimea. In July 1979, 311 *OKShAP* Yak-38s became operational aboard the aircraft carrier *Minsk*. The *Minsk* was stationed at Strelok Bay in the Sea of Japan. Yak-38s also became operational from the *Kiev*-class carrier *Novorossiysk* in September 1982. A total of 231 Forgers were produced, with two primary variants existing– the Yak-38U and the Yak-38M. All Forgers were retired in 1991.

A Soviet Yakovlev Yak-38 Forger in 1985. (US Navy)

Above: A Yak-38 Forger prepares to make a vertical landing in 1986. (US Navy)

Right: Yak-38 Forger Cs aboard the Soviet Navy carrier VHG *Minsk*. (US Navy)

9

The HARRIER LEGACY and the FUTURE of the VSTOL STRIKE FIGHTER CONCEPT

The Hawker Siddeley Harrier served as a modern-day embodiment of Hawker Siddeley's achievement of excellence in aeronautics. The Harrier, the only true successful VSTOL jet strike fighter design, incorporated all of the cardinal Hawker aircraft design principles established long before its time. It demonstrated itself as a highly capable and extraordinary warrior in combat during the Falkland Islands conflict, while its American derivative, the McDonnell Douglas AV-8B, did so as well in Operations *Desert Storm*, *Iraqi Freedom* and *Enduring Freedom*. The Harrier has also distinguished itself in service with the navies of several foreign nations, including Spain, India, Italy and Thailand. A total of 869 Harriers were produced and some are still in service with the USMC.

It is now up to the stealthy Lockheed Martin F-35 Lightning II joint strike fighter to carry on the legacy and tradition of the VSTOL Strike Fighter Concept. The F-35A successfully performed its maiden flight on 15 December 2006 and is now operational with the USMC (F-35B) and USAF (F-35A). The Lightning II will be operational with the US Navy (F-35C) within the next year. The USMC Lightning II variant, the F-35B, makes use of the short take-off and vertical landing (STOVL) concept. The aircraft features a sturdy, stealthy, structural design; advanced, combined avionics and sensor technology; and advanced, high-speed data network systems. The F-35B's powerplants consist of a Pratt & Whitney F135 engine (main engine), which enables the Lightning II to fly at supersonic speeds, and the Rolls-Royce Lift System, which features a lift fan (in the forward fuselage) and a 3BSM thrust vectoring nozzle (deflects main engine exhaust downward), for STOVL operations. The aircraft also features an AN/APG-81 Active electronically scanned array-radar and an Electro-Optical Targeting System (EOTS) positioned on the nose. The USMC Lightning II variant may be armed with an externally mounted GAU-22/A gun pod, either two AIM-9X Sidewinder or AIM 132 ASRAAM short-range air-to-air missiles (AAMs) (carried on two outer pylons), AIM-120 AMRAAM BUR AAMs (carried on inner underwing pylons), AGM-158 Joint Air to Surface Stand-off Missile (JASSM) cruise missiles (carried on other underwing pylons), as well as an array of precision bombs (carried on other underwing pylons). The main operators of the Lightning II will be the United States Air Force, United States Marine Corps, United States Navy, Britain's Royal Air Force and Royal Navy, the Italian Air Force and Navy, the Royal Australian Air Force, the Royal Danish Air Force, the Israeli Air Force, the Japanese Air Self-Defense Force, the Royal Netherlands Air Force, the Royal Norwegian Air Force, the Republic of Korea Air Force, and the Turkish Air Force. It can only be hoped that the Harrier's replacement, the Lockheed Martin F-35 Lightning II, will live up to the legacy left behind by the Hawker Siddeley Harrier.

Left: A USMC Lockheed Martin F-35B Lightning II performs a vertical landing during flight trials aboard the amphibious assault ship USS *Wasp* (LHD 1) on 14 August 2013. (US Navy photo courtesy of Lockheed Martin by Andy Wolfe)

Above: A USMC F-35B test aircraft drops a laser-guided bomb over the flight test range at Naval Air Station Patuxent River, Maryland. (Lockheed Martin by Dane Wiedmann)

Left: A British F-35B in flight over Eglin AFB, Florida, United States, on 21 May 2014. (USAF photo by Staff Sgt Katerina Slivinske)

NOTES

1. RG 255, NACA Classified File 1915–58 1001 Hannovraner thru 1001 Heath, Box 229, Folder 1001 Hawker/2, *Hawker: Aircraft of Achievement*, The H.G. Hawker Engineering Co., LTD, Kingston-on-Thames, England, p. 4. US National Archives at College Park, MD, Textual Reference Branch.
2. Ibid., p. 12.
3. Bader, Douglas. *Fight for the Sky: The Story of the Spitfire and Hurricane*. London: Cassell Military Books, 2004, p. 41.
4. Holmes, Tony. *Hurricanes to the Fore: The First Aces* (Aircraft of the Aces: Men and Legends Ser.# 7). Oxford: Osprey Publishing, 1999, p. 12.
5. Holmes, Tony. *Hurricane Aces, 1939–1940*. Oxford: Osprey Publishing, London, 1998, p. 106.
6. Stores, Christopher and William S. Clive. *Aces High*. London: Neville Spearman, 1966, p. 226.
7. Bader, Douglas. *Fight for the Sky: The Story of the Spitfire and Hurricane*. London: Cassell Military Books, 2004, pp. 165–7.
8. Shores, Christopher, Brian Cull and Yasuho Izawa. *Bloody Shambles: Volume Two: The Defence of Sumatra to the Fall of Burma*. London: Grub Street, 1993, pp. 421–2.
9. 'Obituary of Lt-Cdr Sammy Mearns'. *The Telegraph*, 14 June 2009. Retrieved: 20 September 2010. www.telegraph.co.uk/news/obituaries/military-obituaries/naval-obituaries/5533906/Lt-Cdr-Sammy-Mearns.html.
10. Ramsay, Winston G. (ed.). *The Blitz Then and Now Volume 3: May 1941–May 1945*. London: Battle of Britain Prints International Ltd, 1990, p. 165.
11. Caldwell, Donald. *JG26 Luftwaffe Fighter Wing War Diary: Volume Two: 1943–45*. Mechanicsburg, PA, USA: Stackpole Books, 2012, pp. 15–17.
12. Zetterling, Niklas. Normandy 1944: German Military Organisation, Military Power and Organisational Effectiveness. Canada: J.J. Fedorwicz Publishing Inc., 2000, pp. 38, 52.
13. Grey, Peter and Sebastian Cox. *Air Power: Turning Points from Kittyhawk to Kosovo*. London: Frank Class Publishers, 2002, p. 105.
14. Thomas, Chris. *Typhoon Wings of 2nd TAF 1943–45*. Oxford: Osprey Publishing, 2010, p. 74.
15. Thomas, Chris. *Typhoon and Tempest Aces of World War 2*. Oxford: Osprey Publishing, 1999.
16. Mason, Francis K. *Hawker Aircraft Since 1920 (3rd revised edition)*. London: Putnam, 1991, p. 332.
17. Mason, Francis K. *The Hawker Tempest I–IV* (Aircraft in Profile Number 197). Leatherhead, Surrey: Profile Publications Ltd, 1967, p. 5.
18. Ibid., p. 7.
19. '4-Cannon Tempest Chases Nazi Robot Bomb'. *Popular Mechanics*, February 1945. Retrieved: October 2016. books.google.com/books?id=h98DAAAAMBAJ&pg=PA54&dq=Popular+Science+1930+plane+%22Popular+Mechanics%22&hl=en&ei=eQ6ITrr5CXvOgGmOM3lDw&sa=X&oi=book_result&ct=result&resnum=7&ved=0CEYQ6AEwBjgo#v=onepage&q&f=true.
20. 'Hawker Tempest'. *hawkertempest.se*. Retrieved: 1 January 2012. http://www.hawkertempest.se/.
21. Thomas, Chris and Christopher Shores. *The Typhoon and Tempest Story*. London: Arms and Armour Press, 1988, p. 193.

22. Mason, Francis K. *The Hawker Tempest I–IV* (Aircraft in Profile Number 197). Leatherhead, Surrey: Profile Publications Ltd, 1967, pp. 14, 16.

23 Mackay, Ron. *Hawker Sea Fury in Action*. Carrollton, Texas: Squadron/Signal Publications, 1991, p. 10.

24. Cooper, Tom. 'Clandestine US Operations: Cuba, 1961, Bay of Pigs'. 2007. Retrieved: 18 March 2014. www.acig.info/CMS/index.php?option=com_content&task=view&id=83&Itemid=47.

25. Wheeler, Barry C. *The Hamlyn Guide to Military Aircraft Markings*. London: Chancellor Press, 1992, p. 87.

26. Mason, Francis K. *The Hawker Sea Hawk*. Leatherhead, Surrey: Profile Publications Ltd, 1966, p. 6.

27. Green, William, ed. 'Hawker Sea Hawk: Fighter A-Z'. *Air International*, Vol. 23, No. 1, July 1982, p. 49.

28 Jackson, Robert. *Modern Combat Aircraft 15, Hawker Hunter*. Shepperton, Surrey: Ian Allan, 1982, p. 8.

29. Mason, Francis K. *The British Fighter Since 1912*. Annapolis, Maryland: Naval Institute Press, 1992, p. 368.

30. 'R.Ae.C. Award Winners'. *Flight International*, 5 February 1954. Retrieved: 3 November 2009. www.flightglobal.com/pdfarchive/view/1954/1954%20-%200309.html.

31. Skardon, C. Philip. *A Lesson for Our Times: How America Kept the Peace in the Hungary-Suez Crisis of 1956*. Bloomington, Indiana: AuthorHouse, 2010, p. 478.

32. Fricker, John. MR2 'Nimrod: ASW Specialist'. *Flight International*, 27 April 1972, pp. 593–4. www.flightglobal.com/pdfarchive/view/1972/1972%20-%200999.html?search=nimrod.

33. Neal, Molly. 'Nimrod: Systematic Sub Hunter'. *Flight International*, Vol. 97, No. 3176, 22 January 1970, pp. 119–28. www.flightglobal.com/pdfarchive/view/1970/1970%20-%200147.html.

34. Burden, Rodney A., Michael A. Draper, Douglas A. Rough, Colin A. Smith and David Wilton. *Falklands: The Air War*. Twickenham: British Air Review Group, 1996, pp. 402–3.

35. Chant, Chris. *Air War in the Falklands 1982*. Osprey Publishing, 2001, p. 33.

36. Burden, Rodney A., Michael A. Draper, Douglas A. Rough, Colin A. Smith and David Wilton. *Falklands: The Air War*. Twickenham: British Air Review Group, 1996, p. 403.

37. Lake, Jon. 'New Roles for the Mighty Hunter'. *Air International*, Vol. 69, No. 3. September 2005, pp. 53–4.

38. 'Archived copy'. Archived from the original on 18 June 2009. Retrieved 5 October 2009. 'The Test Flying Memorial Project, British Flight Test Accidents: 1946–1970'. web.archive.org/web/20090618144718/http://www.testflyingmemorial.com/1946-70.html.

39. Mason, Francis K. *The Hawker P.1127 and Kestrel (Aircraft in Profile 93)*. Leatherhead, Surrey: Profile Publications Ltd., 1967, p. 3.

40. 'VTOL Aircraft 1965'. *Flight*, 20 May 1965, p. 769.

41. Jefford, C.G., ed. *The RAF Harrier Story*. London: Royal Air Force Historical Society, 2006, pp. 11–12.

42. Mason, Francis K. *The Hawker P.1127 and Kestrel (Aircraft in Profile 93)*. Leatherhead, Surrey: Profile Publications Ltd., 1967, p. 8.

43. Ibid.

44. Ibid.

45. Mason, Francis K. *Hawker Aircraft since 1920*. London: Putnam Publishing, 1971, p. 372.

46. Mason, Francis K. *The Hawker P.1127 and Kestrel (Aircraft in Profile 93)*. Leatherhead, Surrey: Profile Publications Ltd, 1967, p. 10.

47. Chambers, Mark. 'Developing the World's First Jump-Jet: The Story of How NASA Langley Helped to Save the Harrier Program'. *Air Combat*, May/June 1996, Vol. 24, No. 3, p. 8.

48. Ibid., p. 4.

49. Chambers, Joseph R. *Partners in Freedom: Contributions of the Langley Research Center to U.S. Military Aircraft of the 1990s*, NASA SP 2000–4519. Washington, DC: National Aeronautics and Space Administration, 2000, p. 11.

50. Ibid., p. 20.

51. Evans, Andy. *BAe/McDonnell Douglas Harrier*. Ramsbury, UK: The Crowood Press, 1998, pp. 21–2.

52. Vann, Frank. *Harrier Jump Jet*. New York: Bdd Promotional Book Co., 1990, p. 23.

53. Evans, Andy. *BAe/McDonnell Douglas Harrier*. Ramsbury: The Crowood Press, 1998, p. 60.

54. Bull, Stephen. *Encyclopedia of Military Technology and Innovation*. Westport, Connecticut: Greenwood Publishing, 2004, p. 120.

55. Nordeen, Lon O. *Harrier II: Validating V/STOL*. Annapolis, Maryland: Naval Institute Press, 2006, p. 11.

56. Grove, Eric J. *Vanguard to Trident; British Naval Policy since World War II*. London: The Bodley Head, 1987, pp. 319–20.

57. 'First Flight for Sea Harrier FRS2'. Vol. 10 (No. 13). *Janes Defense Weekly*. 1 November 1988: 767.

58. *Flight International*, 1990, p. 9.

59. Graves, David, 2 April 2002. 'Sea Harrier cuts leave the fleet exposed – The decision to retire the decisive weapon of the Falklands conflict means the navy will have to rely on America for air support'. *The Telegraph*. Retrieved: 1 January 2014. www.telegraph.co.uk/news/1389438/Sea-Harrier-cuts-leave-the-fleet-exposed-The-decision-to-retire-the-decisive-weapon-of-the-Falklands-conflict-means-the-Navy-will-have-to-rely-on-America-for-air-support.-David-Graves-reports.html.

60. Evans, Andy. *BAe/McDonnell Douglas Harrier*. Ramsbury: The Crowood Press, 1998, p. 33.

61. Ibid., pp. 174, 176.

62. Nordeen, Lon O. *Harrier II: Validating V/STOL*. Annapolis, Maryland: Naval Institute Press, 2006, p. 31.

63. Ibid., p. 33.

64. Wilson, Stewart. *Bae/McDonnell Douglas Harrier*. Shrewsbury: Airlife Publishing, 2000, p. 29.

65. Nordeen, Lon O. *Harrier II: Validating V/STOL*. Annapolis, Maryland: Naval Institute Press, 2006, p. 61.

66. Wilson, Stewart. *Bae/McDonnell Douglas Harrier*. Shrewsbury: Airlife Publishing, 2000, p. 29.

67. 'More Than a Few Good Men'. *Los Angeles Times*. Retrieved: 26 January 2016. articles.latimes.com/2002/dec/17/nation/na-wall17.

68. 'AV-8B Harrier Operations". GlobalSecurity.org. Retrieved: 21 April 2010. www.globalsecurity.org/military/systems/aircraft/av-8-ops.html

69. Grant, Rebecca. 'The Air Force says it wants a STOVL F-35. Is it right for today's combat environment? Expeditionary fighter'. *Air Force magazine*, March 2005. Washington, DC: Air Force Association. Vol. 3 (No. 88): 38–42.

70. Duffner, Robert W. 'Conflict In The South Atlantic: The Impact of Air Power'. *Air University Review*, March–April 1984. Retrieved: 31 July 2011. www.airpower.maxwell.af.mil/airchronicles/aureview/1984/mar-apr/duffner.html.

71. Jefford, C.G. (ed.). *The RAF Harrier Story*. London: Royal Air Force Historical Society, 2006, p. 89.

72. Feesey, John D.L. 'V/STOL: Neither Myth nor Promise - But Fact'. *Air University Review*, 50(2). Retrieved: 6 March 2011. books.google.com/books?id=Zlt7e7nJwNEC&printsec=frontcover#v=onepage&q&f=false

73. Nordeen, Lon O. *Harrier II: Validating V/STOL*. Annapolis, Maryland: Naval Institute Press, 2006, p. 87.

74. 'AV-8B Harrier II V/STOL Aircraft'. Boeing. Archived from the original on 17 September 2013. Retrieved: 29 September 2013. web.archive.org/web/20130917031046/http://www.boeing.com/boeing/history/mdc/harrier.page.

75. Nordeen, Lon O. *Harrier II: Validating V/STOL*. Annapolis, Maryland: Naval Institute Press, 2006, pp. 127–8.

76. Cordesman, Anthony H. *The Iraq War: Strategy, Tactics, and Military Lessons*. Washington, DC: Centre for Strategic and International Studies, 2003, p. 333.

77. Ibid., p. 334.

78. news.bbc.co.uk/2/hi/uk_news/3146139.stm.

79. Jenkins, Dennis R. *Boeing/BAe Harrier*. Warbird Tech. 21. North Branch, Minnesota: Specialty Press, 1998, pp. 76–7.

80. Nordeen, Lon O. *Harrier II: Validating V/STOL*. Annapolis, Maryland: Naval Institute Press, 2006, pp. 119–20.

81. Jefford, C.G., ed. *The RAF Harrier Story*. London: Royal Air Force Historical Society, 2006, p. 93.

82. Ibid., p. 95.

83. 'UK combat jets fly to Afghanistan'. BBC News, 24 September 2004. Retrieved: January 2017. news.bbc.co.uk/2/hi/uk_news/politics/3686066.stm.

84. 'RN and RAF Harrier combat ops gear up as Royal Navy crews join the fight against the Taleban'. Ministry of Defence. 5 October 2006. Archived from the original on 26 September 2007. Retrieved: 20 March 2011. https://web.archive.org/web/20070926220724/http://www.mod.uk/DefenceInternet/DefenceNews/MilitaryOperations/RnAndRafHarrierCombatOpsGearUpAsRoyalNavyCrewsJoinTheFightAgainstTheTalebanvideo.htm.

85. 'Defence 2009: A Year in Pictures'. Archived 21 November 2010, Wayback Machine. Ministry of Defence, 24 December 2009. Retrieved: January 2017. https://web.archive.org/web/20100912122112/http://www.mod.uk/DefenceInternet/DefenceNews/PeopleInDefence/Defence2009AYearInPictures.htm.

86. Nordeen, Lon O. *Harrier II: Validating V/STOL*. Annapolis, Maryland: Naval Institute Press, 2006, Appendix A, p. 186.

87. Kapur, Harish (October 1987). 'India's foreign policy under Rajiv Gandhi'. *The Round Table*. Vol. 76 (No. 304): pp. 469–80.

88. Tellis, Ashley J. 'The Naval Balance in the Indian Subcontinent: Demanding Missions for the Indian Navy'. *Asian Survey*. Berkeley, California: University of California Press. Vol. 25 (No. 12): pp. 1186–1213.

89. Gandhi, Jatin (25 December 2007). 'Sea Harrier crashes, pilot safe'. *Hindustan Times*. Retrieved: 4 January 2014. www.hindustantimes.com/india/sea-harrier-crashes-pilot-safe/story-snMRaLMBY1KUBP-58Dgy7KO.html

90. Nordeen, Lon O. *Harrier II: Validating V/STOL*. Annapolis, Maryland: Naval Institute Press, 2006, p. 109.

91. Ibid., p. 148.

92. Kington, Tom (14 December 2011). 'Italy Gives Bombing Stats for Libya Campaign'. *Defense News*. Springfield, Virginia: Gannett Government Media. Archived from the original on 28 July 2012. Retrieved: 27 September 2013. archive.is/qoVl.

93. Cook, Kathleen; LeMond-Holman, Ellen. 'Nations Pursue Joint Program Office to Manage Global Boeing Harrier II Fleet' (Press Release), Boeing, 5 December 2003. Archived from the original on 14 September 2011. Retrieved: 2 August 2011. web.archive.org/web/20110914225239/http://www.boeing.com/defense-space/military/av8b/news/2003/q4/nr_031205m.html.

A USMC AV-8B Harrier II Plus performs a vertical landing aboard
the USS Tarawa (LHA 1) during Exercise Kernel Blitz 2001.
(US National Archives at College Park, MD, Still Pictures Branch)

FURTHER READING

Bader, Douglas. *Fight for the Sky: The Story of the Spitfire and Hurricane*. London: Cassell Military Books, 2004.

Bull, Stephen. *Encyclopedia of Military Technology and Innovation*. Westport, Connecticut: Greenwood Publishing, 2004.

Burden, Rodney A., Michael A. Draper, Douglas A. Rough, Colin A. Smith and David Wilton. *Falklands: The Air War*. Twickenham: British Air Review Group, 1996.

Caldwell, Donald. *JG26 Luftwaffe Fighter Wing War Diary: Volume Two: 1943–45*. Mechanicsburg, PA: Stackpole Books, 2012.

Chambers, Joseph R. *Partners in Freedom: Contributions of the Langley Research Center to U.S. Military Aircraft of the 1990s, NASA SP 2000–4519*. Washington, DC: National Aeronautics and Space Administration, 2000.

Chant, Chris. *Air War in the Falklands 1982*. Oxford: Osprey Publishing, 2001.

Cordesman, Anthony H. *The Iraq War: Strategy, Tactics, and Military Lessons*. Washington, DC: Centre for Strategic and International Studies, 2003.

Evans, Andy. *Bae/McDonnell Douglas Harrier*. Ramsbury: The Crowood Press, 1998.

Grey, Peter and Sebastian Cox. *Air Power: Turning Points from Kittyhawk to Kosovo*. London: Frank Class Publishers, 2002.

Grove, Eric J. *Vanguard to Trident: British Naval Policy since World War II*. London: The Bodley Head, 1987.

Holmes, Tony. *Hurricanes to the Fore: The First Aces* (Aircraft of the Aces: Men and Legends Ser. No. 7). Oxford: Osprey Publishing, 1999.

Holmes, Tony. *Hurricane Aces, 1939–1940*. London: Osprey Publishing, 1998.

Jackson, Robert. *Modern Combat Aircraft 15, Hawker Hunter*. Shepperton, Surrey: Ian Allan, 1982.

Jefford, C.G. ed. *The RAF Harrier Story*. London: Royal Air Force Historical Society, 2006.

Jenkins, Dennis R. *Boeing/Bae Harrier, Warbird Tech 21*. North Branch, Minnesota: Specialty Press, 1998.

Mackay, Ron. *Hawker Sea Fury in Action*. Carrollton, Texas: Squadron/Signal Publications, 1991.

Mason, Francis K., *Hawker Aircraft Since 1920* (3rd revised edition) (London: Putnam, 1991).

Mason, Francis K. *The Hawker Tempest I–IV* (Aircraft in Profile Number 197). Leatherhead, Surrey: Profile Publications Ltd, 1967.

Mason, Francis K. *The Hawker Sea Hawk*. Leatherhead, Surrey: Profile Publications Ltd, 1966.

Mason, Francis K. *The British Fighter Since 1912*. Annapolis, Maryland: Naval Institute Press, 1992.

Mason, Francis K. *The Hawker P.1127 and Kestrel* (Aircraft in Profile 93). Leatherhead, Surrey: Profile Publications Ltd, 1967.

Nordeen, Lon O. *Harrier II: Validating V/STOL*. Annapolis, Maryland: Naval Institute Press, 2006.

Ramsay, Winston G. ed. *The Blitz Then and Now Volume 3: May 1941–May 1945*. London: Battle of Britain Prints International Limited, 1990.

Shores, Christopher, Brian Cull and Yasuho Izawa. *Bloody Shambles: Volume Two: The Defence of Sumatra to the Fall of Burma*. London: Grub Street, 1993.

Skardon, C. Philip. *A Lesson for Our Times: How America Kept the Peace in the Hungary-Suez Crisis of 1956*. Bloomington, Indiana: AuthorHouse, 2010.

Stores, Christopher and William S. Clive. *Aces High*. London: Neville Spearman, 1966.

Thomas, Chris. *Typhoon Wings of 2nd TAF 1943–45*. Botley, Oxford: Osprey Publishing, 2010.

Thomas, Chris. *Typhoon and Tempest Aces of World War 2*. Botley, Oxford: Osprey Publishing, 1999.

Thomas, Chris and Christopher Shores. *The Typhoon and Tempest Story*. London: Arms and Armour Press, 1988.

Vann, Frank. *Harrier Jump Jet*. New York: Bdd Promotional Book Co., 1990.

Wheeler, Barry C. *The Hamlyn Guide to Military Aircraft Markings*. London: Chancellor Press, 1992.

Wilson, Stewart. *Bae/McDonnell Douglas Harrier*. Shrewsbury: Airlife Publishing, 2000.

Zetterling, Niklas. *Normandy 1944: German Military Organisation, Military Power and Organisational Effectiveness*. Canada: J.J. Fedorwicz Publishing Inc., 2000.

The History Press

The destination for history
www.thehistorypress.co.uk